SAINTS ALIVE

SAINTS ALIVE

A Forty-Day Pilgrimage with Heroes of Our Faith

MAXIE DUNNAM

 Seedbed

Printed in the United States of America

Unless otherwise noted, Scripture quotations are taken from the Holy Bible, New International Version®, NIV® Copyright © 1973, 1978, 1984, 2011 by Biblica, Inc.™ Used by permission of Zondervan. All rights reserved worldwide. www.zondervan.com The "NIV" and "New International Version" are trademarks registered in the United States Patent and Trademark Office by Biblica, Inc.™ All rights reserved worldwide.

Scripture quotations marked RSV are taken from the Revised Standard Version of the Bible, copyright © 1946, 1952, and 1971 National Council of the Churches of Christ in the United States of America. Used by permission. All rights reserved.

Scripture quotations marked NKJV™ are taken from the New King James Version®. Copyright © 1982 by Thomas Nelson, Inc. Used by permission. All rights reserved.

Scripture quotations marked KJV are taken from the Holy Bible, King James Version, Cambridge, 1796.

Scripture quotations marked ESV are taken from The ESV® Bible (The Holy Bible, English Standard Version®), copyright © 2001 by Crossway Bibles, a publishing ministry of Good News Publishers. Used by permission. All rights reserved.

Scripture quotations marked NASB1995 are taken from the New American Standard Bible®, Copyright © 1960, 1971, 1977, 1995 by The Lockman Foundation. All rights reserved.

Scripture quotations marked NRSVCE are taken from the New Revised Standard Version Bible: Catholic Edition, copyright © 1989, 1993 the Division of Christian Education of the National Council of the Churches of Christ in the United States of America. Used by permission. All rights reserved.

Page design and layout by PerfecType, Nashville, Tennessee

Cover and back cover image by Jules & Jenny, provided by Wikimedia Commons and licensed under the Creative Commons Attribution 4.0 Generic license

Dunnam, Maxie D.
 Saints alive : a forty-day pilgrimage with heroes of our faith / Maxie Dunnam. – Franklin, Tennessee : Seedbed Publishing, ©2023.

 pages ; cm.

 ISBN: 9798888000069 (paperback)
 ISBN: 9798888000076 (epub)
 ISBN: 9798888000083 (pdf)
 OCLC: 1392288918

 1. Devotional calendars. 2. Christian life--Meditations. 3. Spiritual life—Christianity--Meditations.   I. Title.

BV4510.3.D86 2023   248.4   2023944158

SEEDBED PUBLISHING
Franklin, Tennessee
Seedbed.com

CONTENTS

INTRODUCTION

W ell, bless my soul!"
I haven't heard that exclamation in a long time, but I heard it often in my growing-up years in rural Mississippi. When Momma was surprised or felt good about something, she would exclaim, "Well, bless my soul." She had another expression that she used in conversation when there was confusion or she was feeling helpless to act or even speak: "O Lord, I do pray!" Though I have never heard anyone else use that expression, when my family is remembering and talking about my Momma, often someone will simply speak that word as an affirmation of gratitude, "O Lord, I do pray."

Exclamation words are common in most languages. Who has not heard "good grief" or "holy smoke" or "by jove"? I was surprised when I read that "Saints alive!" along with "By jove!" and "Good grief!" are true exclamations. I've heard "by jove" a bit and "good grief" a lot, but I can't remember hearing anyone use "saints alive" as an exclamation.

I'm discovering how I might use it myself, and that's the title of this book. *Saints Alive!* has been an essential growing experience for me. It was one of those times in my life when I felt the call of God to accept a responsibility in which I knew I would fail unless strengthened and guided by the Holy Spirit. I had begun a ministry for which I was ill-equipped, and I remembered Momma's "O Lord, I do pray."

I was invited by the Upper Room to direct a ministry providing direction and resources for growth in the practice of prayer and giving structure to a united expression of prayer for people around the world. I had told the search team that interviewed me, the fact they were interviewing *me* for this responsibility showed what desperate straits the church was in; I was such a novice in my own prayer life.

Saints alive! I had accepted a job for which I knew I was inadequate. Because of my inadequacy, this responsibility forced me to be more deliberate and disciplined in my personal prayer life and also introduced me to a wider dimension of spirituality than I had known.

I immersed myself in books written specifically about prayer, and soon my discipline expanded to the broader area of spiritual formation.

I became intensely interested in the great devotional classics. The Upper Room had published a collection of little booklets—selections from some of the persons whose writings have endured through the centuries—expressing Christian faith and life and becoming classic resources for pilgrims on the Christian way. Those little booklets, providing selections from twenty-nine of these saints, were packaged in a box together under the label *Great Devotional Classics*. Saints alive! I call it my box of saints.

For more than fifty years that box has set in an obvious place among my books. The box is a bit fragile now because, ever and again through the years, I have taken one of the books out to reread it. Only a few other writers have shaped me more spiritually than those in my box of saints.

During the COVID-19 pandemic, I pulled the box down again. The stay-at-home orders had come; we were in lockdown and it soon became apparent I needed help. I decided that I would live, at least part-time, with some of the saints. Anticipating the lockdown would last at least thirty days, I selected ten of the little booklets in my box, thinking I would live three days with each, and that would get me through the month.

This devotional book is a result of that period of pandemic isolation, written primarily during the time I was living with these particular devotional classics. Later, during Lent, I added other saints to my reflection for forty days. I've arranged it for a reading each day, Monday through Friday, with a word from two or three saints considered during each week. Each day begins with Scripture—because Scripture and prayer are central to all these persons (a lesson within itself)—and closes with a guide for a reflective moment and a prayer.

My prayer is that the forty days you live with these saints will be inspiring and transformative. Perhaps, like me, you will see what rich resources they are for your ongoing spiritual formation. Though my particular box of saints is out of print, you can easily find other books containing the writings of these persons.

DAY 1

Francis de Sales

⸺ ✑ ⸺

Devotion and Discipline

Then Jesus said to his disciples, "Whoever wants to be my disciple must deny themselves and take up their cross and follow me. For whoever wants to save their life will lose it, but whoever loses their life for me will find it. What good will it be for someone to gain the whole world, yet forfeit their soul? Or what can anyone give in exchange for their soul?" (Matt. 16:24–26)

B y way of introducing the meaning of true devotion Francis de Sales wrote:

As ostriches never fly, as hens fly low, heavily, and but seldom, and as eagles, doves, and swallows fly aloft, swiftly and frequently, so sinners fly not at all toward God, but lie groveling on earth with only earthly objects in view.*

---

* Francis de Sales, *Selections from the Introduction to the Devout Life*, arr. and ed. Thomas S. Kepler (Nashville, TN: The Upper Room, 1962), 14–15.

1

Saints alive!

Anyone who has read the Gospels knows that Jesus's call is to a *narrow way* (Matt. 7:13–14). I don't know a Christian in all the ages to whom we turn for teaching and inspiration who did not give himself to discipline and devotion. The nature of this practice is often misunderstood and misguided.

If the Bible had said that you are saved by grace through intelligence, some of us would have been too dumb. If we were saved by grace through looks, some of us would be too ugly. If we were saved through education, some of us would be too ignorant. If we were saved by grace through money, some of us would be too poor. But all that is necessary for you to be saved is simply faith in the Lord Jesus Christ.

Francis de Sales had an inspiring understanding:

> True devotion is a thorough love of God. "For inasmuch as divine love adorns the soul, it is called grace, making us pleasing to the Divine Majesty; inasmuch as it gives us the strength to do good, it is called charity; but when it is arrived at that degree of perfection by which it makes us do well but also work diligently, frequently, and readily, then it is called devotion."[*]

Genuine devotion presupposes the love of God; thus the disciplines we practice must be all for the love of God. This notion is too

---

* De Sales, *Devout Life*, 14.

often not known and is certainly ignored, particularly early in our Christian walk.

> Good people who have not as yet attained to devotion fly toward God by their good works, but rarely, slowly and heavily, but devout souls ascend to Him by more frequent, prompt, and lofty flights.*

As de Sales demonstrates, and as we will see as we reflect on many lessons we learn from the saints, we need to give attention to discipline and devotion for the purpose of enhancing our relationship with Christ, of cultivating a vivid companionship with him. Through discipline and devotion, we learn to be like Christ and to live as He lived.

———————————————— ⌒ ————————————————

REFLECTIVE MOMENT: How have you sought to express devotion and discipline?

PRAYER: God, my Father, I confess I seek to fly toward You by my good works, and it is slow and heavy. Release me from that notion. I want to make frequent, prompt, and lofty flights. Amen.

---

* De Sales, *Devout Life*, 15.

Francis de Sales

⌒

Awareness of God's Presence

Whither shall I go from thy spirit? or whither shall I flee from
   thy presence?
If I ascend up into heaven, thou art there: if I make my bed in
   hell, behold, thou art there.
If I take the wings of the morning, and dwell in the uttermost
   parts of the sea;
Even there shall thy hand lead me, and thy right hand shall hold
   me. (Ps. 139:7–10 KJV)

F rancis de Sales, along with many of the persons from whom,
   through their writings, we have received spiritual guidance
through the centuries, provided personal guidance for particular
persons. Much of this guidance was done through letters. These letters
were either preserved and printed as originally written or edited by
the author or some other person who wanted to make them available.

De Sales took the correspondence he had with Madame Louise de Charmoisy over a number of years, along with spiritual direction he had prepared for her and others, and organized it into the book *Introduction to the Devout Life*. This material was addressed to a lover of God, Philothea, who is to remain in the thick of secular life but would offer her life to God in that situation.* He taught her (and us) how to be aware of God.

We begin by deliberately placing ourselves in the presence of God and imploring His assistance. De Sales sounded four principal means for doing this:

1. Attention to the fact that God is present in all things: "Whither shall I go from thy spirit? or whither shall I flee from thy presence? If I ascend up into heaven, thou art there: if I make my bed in hell, behold, thou art there" (Ps. 139:7–8 KJV). There is no place in which God is not.

2. Not only is God in the place where you are, but He is present in a particular manner in the very center of your spirit.

3. Consider our Savior in His humanity looking down from heaven on all mankind, but especially on Christians, who are His children, and more particular the ones who are praying, whose actions and behavior He minutely observes.

---

* Douglas V. Steere, *Doors to God* (New York: Harper and Brothers, 1948), 59.

4. Use your imagination to picture Jesus near you, as a friend with whom you delight in sharing.[*]

As I reflect on these principal means of de Sales, it is clear that he influenced my definition of spiritual formation—that dynamic process of receiving through faith and appropriating through commitment, discipline, and action the living Christ into our own life to the end that our life will conform to and manifest the reality of Christ's presence in the world.

De Sales urged us to employ some of these four means of putting ourselves in the presence of God as we begin our prayer. As I have employed these principal means in relation to prayer, it has been transformative. I now seek to practice *prayerful living*. I do that, however falteringly and imperfectly, by recognizing, cultivating awareness of, and giving expression to the indwelling Christ. By *recognizing*, I mean more than affirming Christ's presence. Through spiritual disciplines, living with Scripture, worship, meditation and reflection, and intentional conversation with other Christians, we make *cultivating* Christ's presence within us an ongoing process.

Saints alive! . . . There is more. By *giving expression to* the indwelling Christ, I mean actually reflecting His life within us in

---

[*] Francis de Sales, *Selections from the Introduction to the Devout Life*, arr. and ed. Thomas S. Kepler (Nashville, TN: The Upper Room, 1962), 7–9.

our daily living; living out of His presence so that His Spirit will be expressed through us.*

REFLECTIVE MOMENT: Read again the four principal ways we employ for claiming awareness of God. Are you practicing any of these?

PRAYER: Help me, Lord, to see You more clearly, love You more dearly, and follow You more nearly this day. Amen.

---

* Maxie Dunnam, *Alive in Christ* (Nashville, TN: Abingdon Press, 1982), 256.

DAY 3
Francis de Sales

~

Be Meek toward Yourself

"Are not two sparrows sold for a penny? And not one of them
will fall to the ground without your Father's will. But even the
hairs of your head are all numbered." (Matt. 10:29–30 RSV)

What do you think you're worth?

A friend shared this story which deals humorously
with the question of our worth. One day a woman ran out of the
house with the trash when she heard the garbage truck. She wore
a ragged bathrobe and worn-out slippers, her hair was in curlers,
and her face was coated with greasy cream. "Am I too late for the
garbage?" she asked.

"No, hop right in," came the reply.

A man, wrestling with his addiction, pleaded with his pastor,
"Tell me that I'm not a bum. Tell me I'm not junk."

What do you think you are worth? De Sales knew we are
conflicted in thinking about the question. In introducing an

important spiritual practice, he wrote: "We often confess ourselves to be nothing, nay, misery itself, and the refuse of the world; but would be very sorry that any one should believe us, or tell others that we are really so miserable wretches."*

He was teaching about distorted expressions of humility and the need for us to "be meek toward ourselves."

> True humility never makes a show of herself nor uses many humble words . . .
>
> My advice . . . is that we should either not accustom ourselves to words of humility or else use them with a sincere interior sentiment, conformable to what we pronounce outwardly. Let us never cast down our eyes but when we humble our hearts; let us not seem to desire to be the lowest unless we sincerely desire it.†

Christians need to hear his guidance to be meek toward yourself:

> One of the best exercises of meekness we can perform is that of . . . never fretting at our own imperfections; for though reason requires that we should be sorry when we commit any fault, yet we must refrain from that bitter, gloomy, spiteful, and passionate displeasure for which we are greatly to blame,

---

* Francis de Sales, *Selections from the Introduction to the Devout Life*, arr. and ed. Thomas S. Kepler (Nashville, TN: The Upper Room, 1962), 23.
† De Sales, *Devout Life*, 23.

who, being overcome by anger, are angry for having been angry and vexed to see ourselves vexed; for by this means we keep our hearts perpetually steeped in passion; and though it seems as if the second anger destroyed the first, it serves, nevertheless, to open a passage for fresh anger . . .*

It is not what we think of ourselves, or what others think of our worth; it is what God thinks we are worth. Jesus is dramatic in His imaging our worth. He refers to the minimal cost of sparrows: two for a penny! He tells how God knows when one of these almost worthless creatures falls to the ground. Saints alive! Even the hairs on our heads are numbered (Matt. 10:29–30).

The balance is not easy—staying aware of our weakness and failings, sensitive to the fact that we are sinners, and with Paul confessing: "For the good that I would I do not: but the evil which I would not, that I do" (Rom. 7:19 KJV). Paul concluded his honest confession with this vivid assessment and cry: "O wretched man that I am! Who will deliver me from this body of death?" (v. 24 NKJV).

De Sales urged us: be gentle with yourself. Be honest, don't try to cover up, and don't stay there, groveling in your "nothingness." Recognize, confess, and repent. Remember who you are: God's creation, of far more value than a sparrow. Claim the fact Paul claimed as a result of his anguishing question, "Who will deliver me?" "I thank God through Jesus Christ our Lord. . . . There is

---

* De Sales, *Devout Life*, 24.

therefore now no condemnation to them which are in Christ Jesus" (Rom. 7:25a, 8:1a KJV).

Saints alive!

O the bliss of the man who is always angry at the right time and never angry at the wrong time, who has every instinct, every impulse, every passion under control because he himself is God-controlled, who has the humility to realize his own ignorance and his own weakness, for such a man is a king among men!*

REFLECTIVE MOMENT: Do you think of yourself more highly or more lowly than you ought to think?

PRAYER: Lord, keep me humble, but ever mindful that You love me unstintingly. Amen.

---

* William Barclay, "Commentary on Matthew 5," *William Barclay's Daily Study Bible,* https://www.studylight.org/commentaries/eng/dsb /matthew-5.html.

DAY 4
William Law

--- ∽ ---

Centered in God

"From one man he made all the nations, that they should inhabit the whole earth; and he marked out their appointed times in history and the boundaries of their lands. God did this so that they would seek him and perhaps reach out for him and find him, though he is not far from any one of us. 'For in him we live and move and have our being.'" (Acts 17:26–28a)

William Law wrote *A Serious Call to a Devout and Holy Life* over a century after Francis de Sales wrote *The Introduction to the Devout Life*. Both called Christians to distinguish themselves from superficial and shallow expressions of the faith. The church had fallen into a state of mediocrity, its members generally caught in dull spiritual living. It was a lethargic spiritual age in which Law's deep summons for "a serious call to a devout and holy life" was seriously needed. Along with de Sales, he put a strong emphasis on discipline and devotion:

Devotion is neither private nor public prayer; but prayers, whether private or public, are particular parts or instances of devotion. Devotion signifies a life given, or devoted, to God.

He, therefore, is the devout man who lives no longer to his own will, or the way and spirit of the world, but to the sole will of God; who considers God in everything, who makes all the parts of his common life parts of piety, by doing everything in the Name of God, and under such rules as are conformable to His glory.*

Robert Llewelyn titled his collection of daily readings from saints through the year *The Joy of the Saints*. I was inspired by how he described the secret of that joy as a heart wide open to God and stripped of all desire for self-gratification. This is in harmony with Law's contention that the devout person is centered in God. The psalmists stated it often.

> You, God, are my God,
>   earnestly I seek you;
> I thirst for you,
>   my whole being longs for you,
> in a dry and parched land
>   where there is no water.

---

* William Law, *A Serious Call to a Devout and Holy Life*, arr. and ed. Thomas S. Kepler (Nashville, TN: The Upper Room, 1952), 9.

I have seen you in the sanctuary
>   and beheld your power and your glory.
Because your love is better than life,
>   my lips will glorify you.
I will praise you as long as I live,
>   and in your name I will lift up my hands.
I will be fully satisfied as with the richest of foods;
>   with singing lips my mouth will praise you. (63:1–5)

Law reminds us that a life centered in God, wide open to Him, "is a matter of our will, obedience and trust. It is the state of our will that makes the state of our life; when we receive everything from God and do everything for God, everything does us the same good and helps us to the same degree of happiness."*

We may read that casually, but we must not take it lightly. Saints alive! Everything . . . *everything* . . . can and is used by God for our well-being.

During the COVID-19 pandemic, people were asking: "Where is God in all of this?" It seemed easier for people to deal with natural disasters such as hurricanes and tornadoes than with that kind of mysterious invasion. We see those natural disasters as a result of the way the world is. Yet, too many Christians, in relation to the virus, quickly and too easily affirmed: "Well, this is God's will."

---

* Law, *A Serious Call to a Devout and Holy Life*, 51.

There is too much at stake to settle there. Such a response raises too many questions about the nature of God and violates the core witness of Scripture that God is love. As Father, Son, and Holy Spirit, God's goodness and love are limitless. It is like a fresh stream that will flow forever, never drying up. It is beyond God's nature to will for us even a single moment of pain and hurt.

We can live with the mystery of evil and pain if we keep solidly in our minds and hearts that everything that happens is not the will of God, but God has a will in everything that happens. Law expressed it this way: "Sickness and health, prosperity and adversity, bless and purify such a soil in the same degree; as it turns everything towards God, so everything becomes divine to it. For he who seeks God in everything is sure to find God in everything."*

REFLECTIVE MOMENT: In what way, and to what degree, have you found William Law's observation true that "It is the state of our will that makes the state of our life"?

PRAYER: Loving God, enable me to seek You in everything, trusting that I will find You in everything. Amen.

---

* Law, *A Serious Call to a Devout and Holy Life*, 51.

William Law

〜

To Be Meek and Lowly

But I am a worm and not a man,
> scorned by everyone, despised by the people.
All who see me mock me;
> they hurl insults, shaking their heads.
"He trusts in the LORD," they say,
> "let the LORD rescue him.
Let him deliver him,
> since he delights in him." (Ps. 22:6–8)

"Blessed are the meek,
> for they will inherit the earth." (Matt. 5:5)

William Law joined Francis de Sales and most of the classic spiritual teachers in talking about humility.

To be humble in all our actions, to avoid every appearance of pride and vanity, to be meek and lowly in our words, actions, dress, behaviour, and designs, in imitation of our blessed Saviour, is worshipping God in a higher manner than they who have only times to fall low on their knees in devotions. He that contents himself with necessaries, that he may give the remainder to those who want it; that dares not to spend any money foolishly, because he considers it as a talent from God which must be used according to His will, praises God with something that is more glorious than songs of praise.[*]

Meek and *humble* are words often used interchangeably; together and separately they are often distorted and misunderstood. That's one reason Francis de Sales encouraged those he was guiding to be *meek with yourself.*

We think being meek and humble requires self-denial and self-depreciation. To be sure, there is a paramount place in our Christian walk for self-denial, but there is no place for self-depreciation, or any form of devaluing the self. Such misunderstanding of this dimension of the gospel is a limited grasp of true humility. Christian humility is not a groveling "I'll be your doormat" stance.

We have thought of humility only as a recognition and affirmation of weakness and limitation. Not so. The truly humble know who they are—they know their strengths as well as their weaknesses. For this reason, William Law could make the case that we are to use all that we have "as a talent from God which must be used according to

* William Law, *A Serious Call to a Devout and Holy Life*, arr. and ed. Thomas S. Kepler (Nashville, TN: The Upper Room, 1952), 16.

His will." When we do, "it praises God with something that is more glorious than songs of praise."*

We need to note that Paul does not stop after admonishing us not to deceive ourselves by thinking we are something which we are not (Rom. 12:3a). He goes on to urge us to examine ourselves so that we will rejoice in ourselves (v. 3b). We need to learn to affirm strength. Christian character is not to be thought of in terms of weakness, of self-loss, and/or anemic living. To be forgiven and accepted by God, to realize that He knows us thoroughly and loves us thoroughly, to be commissioned, to be made a son/daughter and an heir is to be made a new person in Christ, to be given a vocation. All this means is *to be Christian is to be strong in God, and with God.*

In our theme scripture, the psalmist fell into the pit of self-depreciation, addressing himself as a worm. He moans about how he is mocked and insulted. Note, however, how his enemies respond: "[L]et the LORD rescue him. Let him deliver him, since he delights in him" (Ps. 22:8b). It was redemptive for the psalmist to know, in the midst of his moaning, that the Lord "delights in him." Nothing should delight us more!

REFLECTIVE MOMENT: Do you need to be meek with yourself? Are changes necessary for you to be humble in your actions?

---

* Law, *A Serious Call to a Devout and Holy Life*, 16.

PRAYER: Creator God, forgive me for thinking more highly of myself than I ought. Give me the will and the strength to claim that You delight in me. In the love of Christ, I pray. Amen.

DAY 6
William Law

~

If This Be Your Will

Then Jesus said to them, "Suppose you have a friend, and you go to him at midnight and say, 'Friend, lend me three loaves of bread; a friend of mine on a journey has come to me, and I have no food to offer him.' And suppose the one inside answers, 'Don't bother me. The door is already locked, and my children and I are in bed. I can't get up and give you anything.' I tell you, even though he will not get up and give you the bread because of friendship, yet because of your shameless audacity he will surely get up and give you as much as you need.

"So I say to you: Ask and it will be given to you; seek and you will find; knock and the door will be opened to you. For everyone who asks receives; the one who seeks finds; and to the one who knocks, the door will be opened.

"Which of you fathers, if your son asks for a fish, will give him a snake instead? Or if he asks for an egg, will give him a scorpion? If you then, though you are evil, know how to give good gifts to your children, how much more will your Father in heaven give the Holy Spirit to those who ask him!" (Luke 11:5–13)

P rayer was at the core of the guidance and teaching of all the saints, many offering distinctive teaching. William Law was emphatic about our praying and doing everything wholly for God:

> We readily acknowledge, that God alone is to be the rule and measure of our prayers; that in them we are to look wholly unto Him, and act wholly for Him; that we are only to pray in such a manner, for such things, and such ends, as are suitable to His glory.*

For most of us, it is not a matter of whether we pray, the important issue is *how we pray*. Many of our prayers are simply anemic. We put caveats in them like, "Lord, if it be Your will, then . . ." Too often our prayers sound like we are trying to give God an out or preventing God from being embarrassed. God does not need that.

When I am honest in assessing my praying, when I add "if it is Your will," I am giving myself an out if the prayer is not answered as I intend. Was I praying in faith? Did I really believe God could do what I was asking Him to do? Am I open to God saying no?

I was surprised and helped when somewhere I read this word: "When we get to heaven we will find that many of God's nos were really God's yeses." In hindsight, when we assess our praying, most of us have experienced the relief that comes when God does not

---

* William Law, *A Serious Call to a Devout and Holy Life*, arr. and ed. Thomas S. Kepler (Nashville, TN: The Upper Room, 1952), 9.

answer our prayers in the way we want. That does not mean we are to quit praying! Over a long period, I have come to the place in my life that, when I want something from God, I boldly ask God for it. For me, that means two things: (1) I am more thoughtful in examining my wants, and (2) if God does not want me to have it, then God won't give it to me, and I won't be upset.

God knows what is best, so I can still pray boldly, because God likes bold prayers. The Bible is filled with bold prayers.

Law not only makes the case for all our praying to be "in such a manner, for such things, and such ends, as are suitable to His glory"[*] but also says we are to live our lives in that manner:

> Now let any one but find out the reason why he is to be thus strictly pious in his prayers, and he will find the same as strong a reason to be as strictly pious in all the other parts of his life. For there is not the least shadow of reason why we should make God the rule and measure of our prayers; . . . but what equally proves it necessary for us to look wholly unto God, and make Him the rule and measure of all the other actions of our lives.[†]

---

[*] Law, *A Serious Call to a Devout and Holy Life*, 9.

[†] Law, *A Serious Call to a Devout and Holy Life*, 9.

———————————— ⸌⸍ ————————————

REFLECTIVE MOMENT: How expectant is your praying? What does this say about your confidence in God?

PRAYER: "I surrender, Lord, I give myself to Thee; fill me with Thy love and power, let Thy blessing fall on me."* Amen.

---

* "All to Jesus I Surrender," lyrics by Judson W. Van DeVenter, music by Winfield S. Weeden, 1896, public domain.

DAY 7
François Fénelon

~

Loving Self and Self-Loving

On one occasion an expert in the law stood up to test Jesus. "Teacher," he asked, "what must I do to inherit eternal life?"

"What is written in the Law?" he replied. "How do you read it?"

He answered, "'Love the Lord your God with all your heart and with all your soul and with all your strength and with all your mind'; and, 'Love your neighbor as yourself.'"

"You have answered correctly," Jesus replied. "Do this and you will live." (Luke 10:25–28)

François Fénelon was the archbishop of Cambrai from August 1695 until his death on January 7, 1715. But he is best known for being a great "director of souls." Louis de Rouvroy, Duc de Saint-Simon, wrote of him:

> I have never seen any other person and which, though seen but once, could never be forgotten. . . . One had to make

an effort to cease looking at him. There was, too, a sympathetic merging of his own personality with that of a friend with whom he was speaking, a subtle and inborn grace which made some say, "His friends love him because they see themselves in him."[*]

Knowing even a bit of his giftedness and achievements, it is a sign of Fénelon's honesty and self-knowledge to read this counsel: "The most important thing, if you really wish to be a religious man, is to distrust yourself, after so many proofs of your weakness, and to renounce immediately those companions that might lead you from the right path."[†]

Nor is it a surprise that such a person would write of how to judge one's self:

While we are so imperfect, we can understand only in part. The same self-love that causes our defects injuriously hides them from ourselves and from others. Self-love cannot bear the view of itself. It finds some hiding place; . . . Thus there is always some illusion in us while we are so imperfect and have so much love of ourselves.[‡]

---

[*] Thomas S. Kepler, arr. and ed., *Selections from the Writings of François Fénelon* (Nashville, TN: The Upper Room, 1962), 4.

[†] Kepler, *Writings of François Fénelon*, 9.

[‡] Kepler, *Writings of François Fénelon*, 20.

There is a difference between love of self and self-love. In my more than sixty years in ministry, I have known people whose lives were painfully and purposelessly lived because they did not love themselves; they had such an ugly image of themselves. I have also known people who, loving themselves, made redemptive contributions to others and their community.

Where did we ever get the idea that to love, appreciate, and affirm ourselves is wrong? Certainly we didn't get that from Jesus. When we read the Gospels carefully, we discover that Jesus valued people and called them to step out and use their giftedness in serving others. When He called them to love their neighbors, He gave them the recipe for doing that: "Love your neighbor as yourself" (Mark 12:31). Notice Jesus does not say we are to love our neighbors *instead* of ourselves. We are to love our neighbors *as* we love ourselves.

But self-love is another thing. Self-love is self-centered. Self-centeredness is claiming a place for ourselves which belongs only to God. It is placing ourselves at the center of life and pushing God and others out to the periphery. This is the kind of self-love that Fénelon said must be rooted out.

> Self-love must be uprooted, and the love of God take its place in our hearts before we can see ourselves as we are. Then the same principle enables us to see our imperfections and will destroy them. When the light of truth has risen within us, then we see clearly what is there. Then we love ourselves without particularity, without flattery, as we love

our neighbor . . . in proportion as our strength to support
the view of it increases. We discover our imperfections one
by one as we are able to cure them. Without this merciful
preparation that adapts our strength to the light within . . .*

Of course, we can love ourselves in unhealthy ways, but that is a
problem of kind, not degree. So, it is destructive to love ourselves in the
wrong way, but allowing the love of God to take its place in our hearts,
it is impossible for you to love yourself too much in the right way.

Narcissus, the character from Greek mythology, challenges us.
Narcissus was a youth who was gazing at his reflection in a well one
day. The more he stared, the more enamored of himself he became.
He fell in love with himself, forgot about everything else, tumbled
into the water, and drowned.

It was self-centered loving, and that is always destructive. The
world was created to function in a God-centered way, and nothing will
work out very well until we understand that and cooperate with that.

⌒

REFLECTIVE MOMENT: Examine yourself by answering the
question: Do I love myself too little, too much, or in the wrong way?

PRAYER: Loving Jesus, help me to love myself so that I can love my
neighbor in the right way. Amen.

---

* Kepler, *Writings of François Fénelon*, 20.

DAY 8
François Fénelon

⟶

Loving and Seeking Love

I am writing this not to shame you but to warn you as my dear children. Even if you had ten thousand guardians in Christ, you do not have many fathers, for in Christ Jesus I became your father through the gospel. Therefore I urge you to imitate me. (1 Cor. 4:14–16)

S aints alive! What kind of statement is that? "I urge you to imitate me." If you don't know the setting, it certainly sounds like arrogance.

The word is from Paul in writing to the Corinthian congregation, which was in the midst of a conflict that, if not soon resolved, could destroy the church. The situation was serious. In that congregation some people were critical of the apostle Paul, while others were supportive of him. Some might even have blamed Paul for their present difficulties.

If you read the entire letter, even just the fourth chapter in which his seemingly arrogant request is made, you discover that in the midst of disagreements, Paul's goal was always to build up the church and never to tear it down. His devotion to Christ found him often in trouble, frequently in jail. Trouble and opposition were no strangers to him, but nothing would stop him, certainly not people who were critical of him.

Though dramatic, Paul teaches us about loving, and needing and wanting the love of others. You see often in his writing the tender expression of his gratitude for the love and support of others, confessing how essential it was.

Perspective is a huge factor. Fénelon counsels us here:

> You are willing to give yourself up to others but this makes you an idol to yourself and to them. This is the origin of this refined idolatry of self that God would overthrow in your heart. . . . The sufferings that you complain of spring from yourself. You repulse the hand of God; you listen only to your self-love . . . go where you will, and you cannot escape God's displeasure. . . .
>
> There is no peace except in the destruction of our self-love. You may make some convulsive movements of strength and gaiety, but it is agony that prompts them. If you would make the same effort for the peace of God as you make against it, how unspeakable would be your happiness.[*]

---

* Thomas S. Kepler, arr. and ed., *Selections from the Writings of François Fénelon* (Nashville, TN: The Upper Room, 1962), 30–31.

As we seek the peace of God in relation to dealing with self-love, we must first confess our self-centeredness, yet shamelessly acknowledge *we need the love of others.*

I have a personal witness here. I grew up in rather severe poverty in Perry County, Mississippi. My mother and father did not go to high school. I felt myself culturally, socially, intellectually, and emotionally deprived. In reaction, I developed an inordinate determination to achieve . . . to get out of that situation, to be a success. So I've spent a great part of my life driving myself unmercifully. I've named the game I have played "See here, I am worthy of your love and acceptance."

That has been a distortion of my deep need for the love of others. In expressing that need, we must consider whether it is the *love* or the *praise* of others that we seek. Consider Paul again. The praise of others was not something Paul sought. For him, praise or blame did not matter. He would continue to speak the gospel truth boldly despite the praise or blame he received.

We Christians need to share our faith; we want others to discover for themselves the joy we have found in Christ. There might be times when other people do not want to hear what we have to say, or times when we take a stand based on our faith that is unpopular among our peers. Paul teaches us that as long as we are speaking the truth, it does not matter what other people think of us. We can speak the truth in love without being arrogant. We can share our faith in love without being bigots.

REFLECTIVE MOMENT: Examine your interactions with persons during the past few weeks. Have there been occasions when you related to them in a way that was seeking their praise? Have there been times when you acknowledged your need of their love?

PRAYER: Lord, I need Your love and the love of others. Help me to recognize when persons are offering love, and give me the humility to receive it. Amen.

François Fénelon

⁓

Death, Where Is Your Sting?

When the perishable has been clothed with the imperishable, and the mortal with immortality, then the saying that is written will come true: "Death has been swallowed up in victory."

"Where, O death, is your victory?

Where, O death, is your sting?"

The sting of death is sin, and the power of sin is the law.
(1 Cor. 15:54–56)

All other enemies of humanity are insignificant when contrasted with death. Death breaks up a family circle of loved ones; it leaves an empty place at the dinner table. We can reach the heights of pomp and power, but death brings the mighty to dust and ashes. We can spend years acquiring knowledge and material resources, but death causes all of it to evaporate into nothingness. Death turns life into tragedy. It takes away the meaning of life. If death is the ultimate, then we may just as well "eat and drink [and be merry], for tomorrow we die" (1 Cor. 15:32; cf. Luke 12:19b)! What an enemy!

François Fénelon wrote to a woman who was deeply troubled at the death of her husband:

> It is through great suffering that the mystery of Christianity is accomplished. I mean the crucifixion of self. It is then that the grace of God is unfolded to us and that we understand the intimate operation upon us and that we are taught to sacrifice self. We must turn our thoughts away from ourselves before we can give them to God; . . . it is necessary that our hearts be so deeply wounded that all created things be turned into bitterness to us. Thus touched in the tenderest part, troubled in its sweetest and purest affections, the heart feels that it cannot support itself, and escapes from its weakness and goes to God.
>
> These . . . are violent remedies, but sin has made them necessary. This is the true support of the Christian in affliction. God lays his hand upon two beings united in holy affection. He confers a blessing upon both; he places one in glory, and he makes his removal the means of salvation to the one that remains. This is what God has done for you. May His Holy Spirit awaken all your faith that you may penetrate these truths.*

---

* Thomas S. Kepler, arr. and ed., *Selections from the Writings of François Fénelon* (Nashville, TN: The Upper Room, 1962), 12.

In a brief but clear way, Fénelon made it clear that Christ provides victory over both physical and spiritual death: "He confers a blessing upon both; he places one in glory, and he makes his removal the means of salvation to the one that remains." He gives, victory (glory) over physical death, and salvation over spiritual death. So victory does not belong to death but to persons who die "with Christ" (Rom. 6:8).

Here is what that victory looks like. Bonnie Kittle taught Old Testament literature at Yale Divinity School. She lived with cancer for years, but the students in her classes did not know it.

She came into class one day and lectured on Moses's farewell speech to the nation in the book of Deuteronomy. The class arose and gave her an ovation. Visibly moved, she told everybody to sit down. She told them that this would be her last class with them because she was going to the hospital. They were stunned.

Moses had taken the Israelites through the wilderness for forty years. He wanted now to enjoy the culmination of that pilgrimage and enter the promised land with them. He was not allowed to do so. He accepted that in faith. He faced death as he faced every other moment in his life, trusting in the providence of God. The class saw the parallel. They saw that Bonnie Kittle had lived the same way.

At her memorial service, Leander Keck, dean of Yale Divinity School, spoke: "She bonded with the one on whom death no longer holds a claim. And in her sometimes lonely battle for life, she knew that salvation is nothing if it does not deliver us from death." Saints alive! And then he said this: "*This is the victory of the victim which we celebrate.*"

As Paul wrote, nothing—not even death—can separate us from the love of God or God Himself (Rom. 8:38–39).

Saints alive! Though we physically die, we shall continue to live in and with God. And this is our comfort and hope when we mourn the loss of a loved one.

REFLECTIVE MOMENT: Fénelon claimed that we must turn our thoughts away from ourselves before we can give them to God. To what degree, and in what ways, have you experienced this claim?

PRAYER: I confess, Lord, I am too often self-centered in thought and action. Strengthen me in my will to turn to You. Amen.

DAY 10
Evelyn Underhill

⌒

To Be a Saint

Paul called to be an apostle of Jesus Christ through the will of God, and Sosthenes our brother,

Unto the church of God which is at Corinth, to them that are sanctified in Christ Jesus, called to be saints, with all that in every place call upon the name of Jesus Christ our Lord, both theirs and ours:

Grace be unto you, and peace, from God our Father, and from the Lord Jesus Christ. (1 Cor. 1:1–3 KJV)

Throughout the New Testament, the term *saint* does not primarily refer to the departed dead, and it isn't used exclusively for the holy or the revered. When Paul says "the saints," he means all the believers, all who are called to follow Jesus Christ.

Paul addresses his letter to the Roman Christians: "To all God's beloved in Rome, who are called to be saints" (Rom. 1:7 RSV). He greets the Colossians as "saints and faithful [brothers and sisters]" (Col. 1:2 RSV). He sends his Philippian letter to "all the saints in

Christ Jesus who are at Philippi, with the bishops and deacons" (Phil. 1:1 RSV). And to this Corinthian church, torn by inner divisions, fighting with itself, divided over political and social issues, he still addressed them as "those sanctified in Christ Jesus, called to be saints together with all those who in every place call on the name of our Lord" (1 Cor. 1:2 RSV).

Evelyn Underhill contended that Christians are called to be saints and described them as not "examples of limp surrender. In them we see dynamic personality using all its capacities; and acting with a freedom, originality . . . complete self-loss in the Divine life. In them supremely, will and grace rise and fall together."*

Underhill is far more contemporary than most of the spiritual guides we have been considering. She was born in England in 1875 and died in 1941. Early in her adult life, she developed an immense acquaintance with the Christian mystics, and wrote a huge volume, *Mysticism.* Introducing her in the booklet that is a part of the Upper Room Great Devotional Classics series, Douglas Steere indicated that in 1921 there came a change in her writings.

> Beginning with *Concerning the Inner Life,* one has a sense that she is no longer quoting. What now comes is from the spring that she, too, has known. Her intimate acquaintance with the saints and with the thought and writings of the spiritual guides of the whole sweep of Christian history.†

---

* Douglas V. Steere, arr. and ed., *Selections from the Writings of Evelyn Underhill* (Nashville, TN: The Upper Room, 1961), 12–13.

† Steere, *Writings of Evelyn Underhill,* 5.

I am confident she would smile and affirm Frederick Buechner's description of saints: "the foolish ones and wise ones, the shy ones and overbearing ones, the broken ones and the whole ones, the despots and tosspots and crackpots of our lives who, one way or another, have helped us toward whatever little we may have, or ever hope to have, of some kind of seedy sainthood of our own."*

Her smiling would not diminish her serious consideration and call.

The saints abound in fellowship and service, because they are abandoned to the Spirit, and see life in relation to God, instead of God in relation to life, . . . as material for the expression of Charity. This resort to first principles, this surrender to the priority of the Spirit, and the embodiment of our faith in such meek devotional practice and symbolic action shall stimulate the transcendental sense: this, I believe, is the chief spiritual lack of the modern world.†

We may allow that the saints are specialists; but they are specialists in a career to which all Christians are called. They have achieved, as it were, the classic status. They are the advance guard of the army; but we, after all, are marching the main ranks. The whole army is dedicated to the same supernatural cause; and we ought to envisage it as a whole, and to remember that every one of us wears the same uniform as the saints, has access to the same privileges, is taught

---

* Originally published in *The Sacred Journey* (Harper Row, 1982).
† Steere, *Writings of Evelyn Underhill*, 9.

the same drill and fed with the same food. The difference between them and us is a difference in degree, not in kind.*

The saints have all known that there is no way to be a saint quickly. Francis de Sales gave direction for our beginning journey as saints:

> We must begin with a strong and constant resolution to give ourselves wholly to God, professing to Him, in a tender, loving manner, from the bottom of our hearts, that we intend to be His without any reserve, and then we must often go back and renew this same resolution.†

Underhill would affirm that. Contending that though spiritual achievement might cost much, the cost is never so much as it is worth.

REFLECTIVE MOMENT: Do you consider yourself a saint? Why or why not?

PRAYER: Lord, I want more intentionally to be a saint. Help me to discern the particular price You ask for that of me; help me pay that price, whatever it may be. Amen.

---

* Steere, *Writings of Evelyn Underhill*, 11–12.
† Francis de Sales in *A Year with the Saints: Twelve Christian Virtues in the Lives and Writings of the Saints* (Rockford, IL: TAN Books and Publishers, 2009), 2.

Evelyn Underhill

The Church: A Tool of God to Save the World

For by the grace given me I say to every one of you: Do not think of yourself more highly than you ought, but rather think of yourself with sober judgment, in accordance with the faith God has distributed to each of you. For just as each of us has one body with many members, and these members do not all have the same function, so in Christ we, though many, form one body, and each member belongs to all the others. (Rom. 12:3–5)

E velyn Underhill was not solely concerned about personal spiritual growth. She stayed connected with the established church and counseled about corporate religion. About the nature of the church, she wrote: "The Church is in the world to save the world.

It is a tool of God for that purpose; not a comfortable religious club established in fine historical premises."*

If we are going to actualize the claim that the church is a tool of God to save the world, we must begin courageously practicing the fact that ministry belongs to the whole people of God. As a pastor, I have heard it far too many times: "I am just a layman." Many persons making this statement think they are being asked to do something that a professional Christian is called to do.

"I am just a layman" is irreverent and demeaning. It denies that God has gifted and called all, offering us the incredible privilege of being co-lovers and co-laborers with God in the world. That is clear when we contemplate Paul's New Testament teaching and grasp the image of the church as "the body of Christ." In the section of his teaching on the church as the body of Christ, he closed by naming different functions or particular expressions of vocation: apostles, prophets, evangelists, pastors, and teachers (Eph. 4:11). He listed particular giftings: wisdom, knowledge, faith, healing, working of miracles, prophecy, distinguishing between spirits, speaking in tongues, interpreting tongues, helping, and administration (1 Cor. 12:8–10, 28). Even as early as the New Testament church, there was no effort to eliminate particular functions, the living out of particular gifts and graces.

---

* Douglas V. Steere, arr. and ed., *Selections from the Writings of Evelyn Underhill* (Nashville, TN: The Upper Room, 1961), 21.

The way we sought to express church in the days of the COVID-19 pandemic should have taught us how critical this understanding of ministry is. Without the times of coming together as community for worship, pastors were spending a lot of time and energy seeking ways to keep the sense of caring and community alive. Laypeople were coming alive in these expressions. Notably, one of our church members was diagnosed with an aggressive cancer. A dozen fellow members of his Sunday school class, hearing the news, organized by phone, then went to his home, but did not enter. Practicing social distancing, they surrounded the bedroom area of his house and sang Christian hymns for about twenty minutes.

Think about the mission of the church as saving the world. We have more unsaved and unchurched people in our nation than ever before in our history—more than 172 million. What would happen if the sense of ministry of those dozen people who sang to their friend was cultivated in our congregations?

That ministry belongs to the whole people of God does not mean we will not have orders of ministry. It does mean that we must pay more attention to the calling and anointing of all Christians. Gifts for ministry must have as much consideration as certification.

Underhill counseled that worship was at the center of the mission and ministry of the church:

> I feel the regular, steady, docile practice of corporate worship
> is of utmost importance for the building up of your spiri-
> tual life: more important, really, than advanced books like

De Caussade, though I am delighted that he attracts and helps you and feeds your soul. But no amount of solitary reading makes up for humble immersion in the life and worship of the Church. In fact the books are only addressed to those who are taking part in that life. The corporate and personal together make up the Christian ideal.[*]

She must have been counseling with persons who were having some difficulty with the "institutional church," its life and worship, so she also counseled: "The Church is an 'essential service' like the Post Office, but there will always be some narrow, irritating and inadequate officials behind the counter and you will always be tempted to exasperation by them."[†]

REFLECTIVE MOMENT: As a Christian, do you see yourself as a minister? How are you expressing that?

PRAYER: Father, Son, and Holy Spirit, enlarge my vision of Your church, and enlighten me in being a responsible part of Your body. Amen.

---

[*] Steere, *Writings of Evelyn Underhill*, 22.
[†] Steere, *Writings of Evelyn Underhill*, 22–23.

DAY 12
Evelyn Underhill

◦‿◦

Adoration and Aspiratory Prayer

Pray without ceasing, give thanks in all circumstances; for this
is the will of God in Christ Jesus for you. (1 Thess. 5:17–18 ESV)

Evelyn Underhill was a prominent lay leader in the Anglican
church and a firm proponent of contemplative prayer. Here she
writes of how prayer connects us to God.

A man of prayer is not necessarily a person who says a
number of offices, or abounds in detailed intercessions; but
he is a child of God, who is and knows himself to be in the
deeps of his soul attached to God, and is wholly and entirely
guided by the Creative Spirit in his prayer and his work. This
is not merely a bit of pious language. It is a description, as
real and concrete as I can make it, of the only really apostolic

life. Every Christian starts with a chance of it; but only a few develop it.*

I resonate with Underhill's counsel, especially about persons of prayer knowing in the depths of their soul that they are "attached to God, and [are] wholly and entirely guided by the Creative Spirit in [their] prayer and [their] work." My experience also verifies her judgment that: "Every Christian starts with a chance of it; but only a few develop it."

I became a Christian in my mid-teens and responded to God's call to preach a few years later. I received what was called a "local preacher's license" when I was seventeen. However, it was not until I had finished my seminary training and was serving as a pastor that I began to be serious about prayer. I was happily involved in planting a new Methodist congregation in Gulfport, Mississippi, and, by all traditional standards, was successful. But then my life and ministry took a marked turn. The civil rights movement of the early sixties, and the turmoil and tension that brought to my pastoral leadership, forced something from me that I did not have. Thankfully, prayer and Scripture study became more the center of my life than ever before. I began to structure the congregation around study, prayer, and sharing groups where people became accountable to one another for spiritual growth.

---

* Douglas V. Steere, arr. and ed., *Selections from the Writings of Evelyn Underhill* (Nashville, TN: The Upper Room, 1961), 14.

One principle I learned in that period has become clearer through the years: prayer is the continuing source of power to be obedient in love. Saints alive! Our discipleship, our dynamic for witness, moves on this center—obedience in love. How much of our fervor as Christians is dependent upon the circumstances in which we find ourselves? Yet, prayer is that source of strength enabling us to rise above circumstance.

Discussing this dynamic of persons of prayer knowing in the depths of their soul that they are "attached to God and [are] wholly and entirely guided by the Creative Spirit in [their] prayer and [their] work," Underhill said the laity distinguish in a moment the clergy who have it and those who don't. Then she wrote:

> It is only through adoration and attention that we can make our personal discoveries about Him. . . . I think that if you have only as little as half hour to give each morning to private prayer, it is not too much to make up your minds to spend half that time in such adoration. . . .
>
> I am certain that we gradually and imperceptibly learn more about God by this persistent attitude of humble adoration, than we can hope to do by any amount of mental exploration. For in it our soul recaptures, if only for a moment, the fundamental relation of the tiny created spirit with its Eternal Source; and the time is well spent in getting this relation and keeping it right. In it we breathe deeply the atmosphere of Eternity. . . . We realize, and re-realize, our

tininess, our nothingness, and the greatness and steadfastness of God.*

Underhill's counsel is working itself in my life as I have claimed the fact that prayer is the basic identification we have with the world and with God. Saints alive! Prayer is not just the basic identification we have with God; it's the basic identification we have with the world. Christian prayer destroys our false desire either to be independent of other people or independent of God. Clarence Jordan paraphrased Paul's great word "God was in Christ reconciling the world to Himself" (2 Cor. 5:19 NKJV) in a vivid symbol: "God was in Christ putting his arms around the world and hugging it to himself."†

That's what we do when we pray. We put our arms around another person, we put our arms around a situation, we put our arms around the church, we put our arms around the world, and we hug it to ourselves. And we hug it to God. In some mysterious way that we may never understand, when we pray for another, we are united to that person, and we also become a channel through which God's grace and power flow into the life of that person.

I have learned through the years a form of prayer which, in a way, gives instantaneous momentary expression to all types of prayer. Underhill calls it *aspiratory prayer.*

---

* Steere, *Writings of Evelyn Underhill*, 14.
† Clarence Jordan, *Clarence Jordan's Cotton Patch Gospel: Paul's Epistles* (Macon, GA: Smyth & Helwys Publishing, 2004), page unknown.

[This is the] frequent and attentive use of little phrases of love and worship, which help us, as it were, to keep our minds pointing the right way, and never lose their power of forming and maintaining an adoring temper of the soul. . . . They stretch and re-stretch our spiritual muscles; and, even in the stuffiest surroundings, can make us take deep breaths of mountain air. The habit of aspiration is difficult to form, but once acquired exerts a growing influence over the soul's life. . . . The most important thing in prayer is never what we say or ask for, but our attitude towards God.*

REFLECTIVE MOMENT: Does your praying reflect the validity of Underhill's claim: "The most important thing in prayer is never what we say or ask for, but our attitude towards God"?

PRAYER: Loving Lord, take from me all that hinders my praying. Through Your Holy Spirit instruct me in how to pray. Amen.

---

* Steere, *Writings of Evelyn Underhill*, 18–19.

DAY 13
Bernard of Clairvaux

⌒⌒

True Piety

"Be still, and know that I am God;
   I will be exalted among the nations,
   I will be exalted in the earth." (Ps. 46:10)

Bernard of Clairvaux was born in East Central France in 1090. He had every educational advantage and early showed great promise as a leader and scholar. His conversion to an all-out commitment to God came as he approached his twentieth birthday shortly after his mother's death, when he had set out on a military expedition. He became a part of a religious community at Clairvaux, and it was there that his own inner life of prayer was shaped and deepened.

His preserved writings have come from sermons first preached to the monks in his community in Clairvaux. From there he began many journeys, called on by church and state leaders to be present at their councils to lend his spiritual authority and insight to the profound conflicts of the day.

Introducing him in the Upper Room's Great Devotional Classics series, Douglas Steere wrote:

> In a day when prayer is widely regarded as a subjective exercise which man initiates and where for a brief period a man welcomes God as his guest, an encounter with Bernard of Clairvaux's writings will be a bracing contrast. For instead of man being the host and God the guest, Bernard reverses the role and shows the prevenient God as the host who in prayer initiates in His guest what He later crowns.[*]

When I read that, as a part of the Methodist/Wesleyan expression of the church, I think immediately of John Wesley's description of how grace expresses itself in our life: prevenient, justifying, and sanctifying. *Prevenient grace* is the grace of God going before us, pulling us, wooing us, seeking to open our minds and hearts, and eventually giving us grace. It is the expression of grace expressed by the hymn writer: "I sought the Lord, and afterward I knew He moved my soul to seek Him, seeking me. It was not I that found, O Savior true; no, I was found of Thee."[†]

---

[*] Douglas V. Steere, arr. and ed., *Selections from the Writings of Bernard of Clairvaux* (Nashville, TN: The Upper Room, 1961), 5.
[†] Jean Ingelow, "I Sought the Lord," 1878, public domain.

It is no coincidence, then, that the first entry in *Selections from the Writings of Bernard of Clairvaux* begins with a definition of *piety*:

Do you ask what piety is? It is leaving time for consideration. You may perhaps tell me that herein I differ from him who defines piety as "the worship of God." I do not differ really from him. . . . What is so essential to the worship of God is the practice to which He exhorts in the Psalm, "Be still and know that I am God." This certainty is the chief object of consideration. Is anything, in all respects, so influential, as consideration? . . . [Consideration] purifies the very fountain, that is the mind, from which it springs. Then it governs the affections, directs our action, corrects excesses, softens the manner, adorns and regulates the life, and lastly bestows the knowledge of things divine and human alike.[*]

As *consideration* becomes a spiritual discipline, we begin to live deliberately. I have translated that into three dimensions. The first is *attention*. Jesus talked about men seeing but not really seeing, of hearing but not really hearing (Matt. 13:13–15). This is where many of us are. We're like the American tourist in Paris who rushed into the Louvre and shouted, "Quick, where's the *Mona Lisa*, I'm double-parked outside." We flip through the pages of the Bible, we drop in on church now and then, we offer a quickie prayer as we fall asleep at night and feel that we have performed our religious duties. We have

---

* Steere, *Writings of Bernard of Clairvaux*, 7.

become so conditioned and calloused by science and technology, we have so given ourselves to the reign of law and invariable natural order, that we repudiate even the possibility of some deeper meaning hidden beneath the surface of all the things we observe and measure, but really fail to see.

We reach back into the Old Testament and get the classic story of a person giving attention: the story of Moses and the burning bush. We've heard the story of the burning bush all our lives and yet most of us have not gotten the message. The ongoing burning bush isn't the message; the burning bush was God's way to get Moses's attention.

The second element is *reflection.* Saints alive! It was not enough for Moses to see, he had to *attend* to what he saw. This is the business of *reflection.* It was the decision to look closer that made the difference. The wording of the story is not accidental. The scripture says, "When the Lord saw that [Moses] turned aside to see . . ." (Ex. 3:4 RSV). God called to him out of the burning bush. It was when Moses attended to what he saw that God spoke to him. The height of the mystery is Moses's response to the happening. The scripture goes on to say, "Moses hid his face, for he was afraid to look at God" (v. 6 RSV).

The root of the word *mystery* is a Greek word meaning literally "to shut one's mouth." This is a part of reflection. To shut one's mouth that God might speak. So the psalmist urges to "be still, and know" (Ps. 46:10), to take off our shoes, for the ground on which we stand is holy.

God comes to us in the common events of the day; He also comes to us in those deliberate disciplines of worship, prayer, sharing together in fellowship, studying, and service. Our task is to shut up, to be quiet and reflect, that we may ascertain what He is seeking to communicate. Reflection is the practice necessary for deciphering God's Word in the experience that is ours. We can be sure that the experience of the burning bush was never lost from Moses's memory; more searing than the flames that leaped from the bush was the fire that burned in Moses's soul as he reflected upon that episode.

Reflection means more than seeing clearly and deeply; it means a readiness to respond to what God is saying and where He may be leading. We deliberately, self-consciously, and purposefully open ourselves to some event or some experience to see what God is saying to us.

If we follow up on attention and reflection to live deliberately, there comes the third element: *involvement*.

We often hear someone referring to another as "being his own man." I like to think of Jesus in that fashion. He was His own man. He had the power to take His life up, and He had the power to lay it down. As a model, there is another dimension to Jesus's life that must not be overlooked. He was His own man, but He was His own man *for others.* He possessed a fantastic inner freedom which allowed Him to be the man for others. To be in control of our lives is not to keep ourselves for ourselves, but to give ourselves away for the sake of our brothers and sisters. This is what Jesus meant when He said,

"Greater love hath no man than this, that a man lay down his life for his friends" (John 15:13 KJV).

REFLECTIVE MOMENT: Look back through your life. Can you locate a burning bush experience? How did you respond? If you had a burning bush experience today, would you respond differently?

PRAYER: "Open my eyes, that I may see glimpses of truth Thou hast for me;

place in my hands the wonderful key that shall unclasp and set me free.

Silently now I wait for Thee, ready, my God, Thy will to see;

open my eyes, illumine me, Spirit divine!"* Amen.

---

* The text of the prayer is the first verse of the hymn "Open My Eyes, That I May See" written by Clara H. Scott in 1895.

DAY 14
Bernard of Clairvaux

༄

A Gracious God

When he was at the table with them, he took bread, gave thanks, broke it and began to give it to them. Then their eyes were opened and they recognized him, and he disappeared from their sight. They asked each other, "Were not our hearts burning within us while he talked with us on the road and opened the Scriptures to us?" (Luke 24:30–32)

M artin Luther King Jr. lives in the memory of people around the world, especially in the United States. His birthday is a national holiday in America, a day when US citizens celebrate his commitment to civil rights and nonviolence. We too often forget that King's contribution to American life was solidly rooted in his deep personal faith. In his article "Pilgrimage to Nonviolence," King wrote: "I have . . . become more and more convinced of the reality of a personal God.'"* He confessed that there was a time when God was little more than an interesting topic for theological or philosophical debate. That changed. He experienced God personally, and the reality of God's presence in his life was validated in the everyday pressure and tension of the struggle in which he became engaged. He wrote: "In the midst of the outer dangers I have felt an inner calm and known resources of strength that only God could give."[†]

King's witness confirms the witness of countless Christian leaders. In my journey of keeping company with the saints, I have identified ten characteristics they had in common. The first two of these are: (1) they passionately sought the Lord, and (2) they discovered a gracious God.

Bernard of Clairvaux witnesses to this and counsels us about the nature of God:

> If you say that God is good, great, blessed, wise or any such thing, the starting point is this—*God is* . . . What is God? He is almighty will moved by loving kindness, virtue, eternal light, incommunicable reason, highest blessedness; He is the creator of minds to enjoy Himself; He endows them to long for Him, enlarges them to receive Him, justifies them to

* Martin Luther King Jr., "Pilgrimage to Nonviolence," *Christian Century*, April 13, 1960, https://www.christiancentury.org/article/pilgrimage-nonviolence.

† King, "Pilgrimage to Nonviolence."

be worthy of Him, fires them with zeal, fertilizes them that they may bear fruit, guides them into sweet reasonableness, molds them to loving kindness, regulates them for wisdom, strengthens them for virtue, visits them for consolation, illuminates them for knowledge, preserves them for happiness, is about their path for safety.*

He makes this overwhelmingly beautiful description of God very personal, saying, "How often has the prayer began, almost despairing of salvation, sent me back full of joy and confident of pardon!"†

He speaks of more than receiving gracious pardon. He speaks of how God ministers to us, referring to those who journeyed with a "stranger" on the road to Emmaus after the crucifixion:

[A] Fellow-traveler whose conversation so rejoices them and takes away their weariness that, when He goes, they say, "Did not our hearts burn within us . . . when He talked to us along the way?" He deals thus in His compassion with souls whose hearts are weary of spiritual exercises, have grown dry and sad and turned back on the things of time. He who is from heaven meets us, when we are like this, on our way, and begins to speak of heaven, to sing some lovely

* Douglas V. Steere, arr. and ed., *Selections from the Writings of Bernard of Clairvaux* (Nashville, TN: The Upper Room, 1961), 8, italics in original.
† Steere, *Writings of Bernard of Clairvaux*, 9.

song of Sion [Zion] to us, it may be, or tell us of the peace, the endless peace, that obtains ever in the City of God.*

In seeking God, the saints challenge us to act like travelers who do not regard the road they have traveled or the distance they have come but only look to what lies ahead. Likewise, we must keep our destination before our eyes, even to the journey's end.

Five centuries before Martin Luther King Jr., the person for whom he was named, Martin Luther, the father of the Reformation, shared about a personal experience of God: "I am seeking, searching, thirsting for nothing else than a gracious God."†

Both Martins discovered that's who God is—gracious, seeking us even before we seek Him. Likewise, Bernard of Clairvaux wrote:

It is so important for every soul among you who is seeking to realize that God was first in the field, and was seeking you, before you began to search for Him . . . [T]here is no worse crime than to take to yourself the credit for even a little of the grace one has received. You could not have sought the Word . . . if He had not sought you.‡

---

* Steere, *Writings of Bernard of Clairvaux*, 9–10.

† James Atkinson, ed., *Daily Readings with Martin Luther* (Springfield, IL: Templegate Publishing House, 1949), 48.

‡ Steere, *Writings of Bernard of Clairvaux*, 10–11.

REFLECTIVE MOMENT: Our spiritual guides voice all sorts of descriptive words and images to describe God. In relation to your personal experience of God, what descriptive words or images come to mind?

PRAYER: Ever-seeking God, quicken my recognition, and keep my awareness constant, that I cannot depend on my own resources. Amen.

DAY 15
Bernard of Clairvaux

ɔ

The Cup of Salvation

What shall I return to the LORD
    for all his goodness to me?

I will lift up the cup of salvation
    and call on the name of the LORD.
I will fulfill my vows to the LORD
    in the presence of all his people. (Ps. 116:12–14)

In this passage, the psalmist was in the temple, presenting a thanksgiving offering. The cup of salvation probably referred to an offering of wine that was associated with virtually all animal sacrifices. The worshipper would have lifted up a cup of wine in worship and then would have poured it into a large bowl by the altar as a libation.

Centuries later, Jesus gave a different meaning when He talked about the cup. On the night before His death, He prayed: "O my

Father, if it be possible, let this cup pass from me" (Matt. 26:39 KJV). Here the cup meant the pain and humiliation of crucifixion.

There were several cups that Jesus was offered at Calvary. There was the cup of *charity*. He was offered wine mingled with myrrh to deaden the pain, but He rejected it (Mark 15:23). There was the cup of *mockery*, for the soldiers offered him sour wine (Luke 23:36). There was the cup of *sympathy*, the vinegar that was put on a sponge to moisten his lips (John 19:29).

Earlier, the evening before Calvary, He had handed another cup to His disciples and said, "Drink from it, all of you. For this is My blood of the new covenant" (Matt. 26:27–28 NKJV).

It is natural when Christians come to celebrate the sacrament of the Lord's Supper with bread and wine to consider the chalice of wine as the *cup of salvation*. Bernard wrote of it in this fashion: "I must be grateful, then, for all God's gifts. But there is something that kindles and moves me even more. It is the cup that Thou didst drink, Lord Jesus, more than ought else, that renders Thee love-worthy; it is the work of our redemption that supremely claims our love."*

Scripture and the Christian faith are all about salvation. Salvation began at the beginning. Saints alive! God the Father Almighty, Maker of heaven and earth, loves us so much that He does not forsake us when we go astray.

---

* Douglas V. Steere, arr. and ed., *Selections from the Writings of Bernard of Clairvaux* (Nashville, TN: The Upper Room, 1961), 12.

Again, Bernard wrote:

The Creator bestowed not so much labor on making the whole world, as did our Saviour in redeeming us! In the first work "He spoke and it was done"; but in the second, He put up with people who tried to catch Him in His talk, carped at His actions, mocked His sufferings and even upbraided Him in death. Moreover He was not returning any love of ours in this; but as St. John says, "Not that we loved God, but that He first loved us."

This love of His is tender, wise and strong. Tender in that He took on Him our flesh; careful and wise in that He guarded it against sin; and strong in that He suffered death. It is a thing beyond all measure to look upon man's Maker as a Man . . . I trust myself entirely to Him who willed to save me, knew the way to do it, and had the power to carry out the work. He has sought me out and called me by His grace. . . .*

Think again of the cup. When Jesus came to Calvary, He was offered the same narcotic that the two thieves were offered. Apparently they took it, but He did not. He did not want his senses to be stupefied in any way. He wanted to be in perfect control of His faculties, and to bear the full pain of our pardon. He was going to

---

* Steere, *Writings of Bernard of Clairvaux*, 12–13.

drink the cup of God's radical love dry to the last drop. Again, He can look us in the eyes today and say, "My body given for you; My blood shed for you."

REFLECTIVE MOMENT: Can you say with Bernard, "He has sought me out and called me by His grace"?

PRAYER: "O Jesus, ever with us stay; make all our moments calm and bright. From the best bliss that earth imparts, we turn unfilled to you again."*

---

* Attributed to Bernard of Clairvaux.

DAY 16
Saint Francis of Assisi

∽

Servant above All

I appeal to you therefore, brothers [and sisters], by the mercies of God, to present your bodies as a living sacrifice, holy and acceptable to God, which is your spiritual worship. Do not be conformed to this world, but be transformed by the renewal of your mind, that by testing you may discern what is the will of God, what is good and acceptable and perfect. (Rom. 12:1–2 ESV)

Saint Francis of Assisi is probably the best-known saint. Most are familiar with this prayer that is often attributed to him: "Lord, make me an instrument of your peace." In checking recently, I discovered at the time of my writing that 27.9 million searches about that prayer had been made on Google.

Saint Francis was again called to the attention of the world when Cardinal Jorge Mario Bergoglio was elected pope in 2013. Bergoglio's close friend, Brazilian Cardinal Cláudio Hummes, was sitting with him in the conclave when the vote was moving toward electing him.

His "great friend" comforted him. Then when the vote needed for election was announced, Cardinal Hummes "hugged me, kissed me, and said: 'Don't forget the poor!'"[*]

Later, Bergoglio shared with journalists that, as pope, he took the name Francis because Saint Francis of Assisi was the personification of love and peace, and ardently and sacrificially committed to the poor.

In his youth Francis gave no promise of such a life. He was born in the Italian town of Assisi as the son of a prosperous cloth merchant and reared in carefree comfort. As a young man he shared the dominant ideas of a career in which "wealth, gaiety, romance, and military prestige would be blended to the full measure of enjoyment."[†] But seeking and achieving that did not bring meaning. During his quest for knowledge of God's plan for his life, he soon realized the fact that peace and power came in proportion as he sought more earnestly to imitate the life of Jesus. He resolved to devote his life to the absolute and literal obedience of the commands of Jesus, renouncing possessions, ties of family, and former dreams of worldly success. Henceforth he would take Lady Poverty as his bride.[‡]

---

[*] Salvatore Cernuzio, "Cardinal Hummes, Known as a Defender of the Poor, Dies at 87," *Vatican News*, July 4, 2022, https://www.vaticannews .va/en/vatican-city/news/2022-07/cardinal-hummes-defender-poor -death-brasil.html.

[†] J. Minton Batten, arr. and ed., *Selections from the Writings of St. Francis of Assisi* (Nashville, TN: The Upper Room, 1952), 5–6.

[‡] Batten, *Writings of St. Francis of Assisi*, 5–7.

In his "Letter to All the Faithful," he wrote:

> We ought to observe the precepts and counsels of our Lord
> Jesus Christ. We ought to deny ourselves and to put our
> bodies beneath the yoke of servitude and holy obedience
> as each one has promised to the Lord. And let no man be
> bound by obedience to obey any one in that where sin or
> offence is committed.*

What God asks us is a will which will no longer be divided. The
road leading to God does not entail a multiplicity of considerations,
methods, manners, and experiences... but demands only the one thing
necessary: true self-denial, exterior and interior, through yielding of
self both in surrender to and suffering for Christ in all things.

> We should never desire to be above others, but ought rather
> to be servants and subject "to every human creature for
> God's sake." And the spirit of the Lord shall rest upon all
> those who do these things and who shall persevere to the
> end, and He shall make His abode and dwelling in them,
> and they shall be children of the heavenly Father, whose
> works they do ...†

Paul, in his word to the Romans, made it clear: "I urge you,
brothers and sisters, in view of God's mercy, to offer your bodies as

---

* Batten, *Writings of St. Francis of Assisi*, 26–27.
† Batten, *Writings of St. Francis of Assisi*, 27.

a living sacrifice, holy and pleasing to God—this is your true and proper worship" (Rom. 12:1). Our problem is we want to baptize our old nature, rather than trade it in. We're not told to wash the old nature, however, but to kill it. True Christianity is a state in which we are utterly, absolutely, and completely surrendered to God.

Genuine Christian living is not defined by how happy we are, how prosperous or healthy we are, or even by how many people we have led to the Lord in the last year. Christian health is ultimately defined by how sincerely we wave our flag of surrender.

The questions leading to spiritual growth and health, then, are: What is God's will for me in this hour and day? Where is God leading me? How can I surrender to Him?

In charming and challenging use of imagery, Francis says:

[We] are the spouses, brothers and mothers of our Lord Jesus Christ. We are spouses when by the Holy Ghost the faithful soul is united to Jesus Christ. We are His brothers when we do the will of His Father who is in heaven. We are His mothers when we bear Him in our heart and in our body through pure love and a clean conscience and we bring Him forth by holy work which ought to shine as an example for others.*

---

* Batten, *Writings of St. Francis of Assisi*, 27–28.

REFLECTIVE MOMENT: The Christian faith is defined by how sincerely we wave the flag of surrender. What present meaning does this have in your life?

PRAYER: Lord Jesus, I confess, my will is weak. I will surrender only by the power of the Holy Spirit. Give me that power. Amen.

Saint Francis of Assisi

Praise the Lord

Praise the LORD.

Praise God in his sanctuary;
    praise him in his mighty heavens.
Praise him for his acts of power;
    praise him for his surpassing greatness.
Praise him with the sounding of the trumpet,
    praise him with the harp and lyre,
praise him with timbrel and dancing,
    praise him with the strings and pipe,
praise him with the clash of cymbals,
    praise him with resounding cymbals.

Let everything that has breath praise the LORD.

Praise the LORD. (Ps. 150)

After voicing all the ways that we should praise the Lord, the psalmist concluded, "Let everything that has breath praise the LORD." I doubt if anyone has taken that more literally than Saint Francis. He was explicit in addressing his praise to the three persons of the Trinity:

> Worthy art Thou, O Lord, our God, to receive praise, glory and honor and benediction. Let us praise and exalt Him above all forever.
>
> The Lamb that was slain is worthy to receive power and divinity and wisdom and strength and honor and benediction. Let us praise and exalt him above all forever.
>
> Let us bless the Father and the Son with the Holy Ghost. Let us praise and exalt Him above all forever. . . .
>
> Let the heaven and earth praise Him, the Glorious, and every creature which is in heaven and on earth and under the earth, in the seas and all that are in them.*

People who don't consider the depth and expanse of Francis's explicit Christian teaching exalt what they consider pantheistic. His "Canticle of the Sun" is one of his most well-known writings. He began, "Praise be my Lord with all His creatures; and specially our brother the sun, who brings us the day, and who brings us the light;

---

* J. Minton Batten, arr. and ed., *Selections from the Writings of St. Francis of Assisi* (Nashville, TN: The Upper Room, 1952), 29–30.

fair is he, and shining with a very great splendor: O Lord, he signifies to us Thee!"*

In the canticle, he goes on to praise our brother, the wind; our sister, the water; our brother, fire; then he becomes even more expansive: "Praise be my Lord for our mother, the earth, the which doth sustain us and keep us, and bringeth forth divers fruits and flowers of many colours, and grass."†

This is far, far from pantheism, and certainly not anywhere close to nature worship. Nature worship is often considered the primitive source of modern religious beliefs, and can be found in theism, pantheism, deism, polytheism, animism, and even paganism. Saint Francis's images of things are not God, but God is in all things. Paul was suggesting this when he wrote: "And we know that in all things God works for the good of those who love him" (Rom. 8:28a).

"The Canticle of the Sun" becomes deeply meaningful, and calls us to worship in the midst of the natural world, as we keep in mind how he referred to "our brother the sun . . . shining with a very great splendor: O Lord, he signifies to us Thee!"

In many ways, Wendell Berry is a modern-day Saint Francis. He is the author of more than eighty books of poetry, fiction, and essays. When he went to teach at the University of Kentucky, he and his wife made the decision they would not live in the city but, rather, in the country. They bought an old house and twelve acres, and moved in

---

* Batten, *Writings of St. Francis of Assisi*, 31.
† Batten, *Writings of St. Francis of Assisi*, 32.

as it was being renovated in the summer of 1965. They had children and raised them there, and now they have grandchildren who are at home there. His poetry is often political commentary, reflection on contemporary issues, championing the values of nature and rural life. More than anything, it is a celebration of the whole of creation in a Franciscan kind of way. In his poem "Meditation in the Spring Rain," he writes: "The thickets, I said, send up their praise at dawn!"*

I imagine that, along with Saint Francis, Psalm 150 is Berry's favorite psalm. His writing and Saint Francis's "Canticle of the Sun" call to mind that psalm: "Let everything that has breath praise the LORD" (v. 6a).

When his faith was at its lowest point, G. K. Chesterton said that he maintained it by gratitude toward God. He said he hung on "the remains of religion by one thin thread of thanks."

Saints alive! Praise and thanksgiving belong not to a particular day or a particular season, but to the whole of life. "Praise the LORD! Praise God in His sanctuary; Praise Him in His mighty firmament!" (Ps. 150:1 NKJV).

REFLECTIVE MOMENT: One of my favorite hymns, "All Creatures of Our God and King" is the canticle set to music. Reflect on the

---

* Wendell Berry, *Collected Poems* (San Francisco: North Point Press, 1988), 135.

last stanza: "Let all things their Creator bless, and worship Him in humbleness . . . Praise, praise the Father, praise the Son, and praise the Spirit, Three in One."*

Now, pray that last line of praise.

How do you experience nature? Do you tend to make the things of nature sacred to be worshipped, or do you recognize God in all His creation and worship Him?

PRAYER: "Praise, praise the Father, praise the Son, and praise the Spirit, Three in One." Thank you, Lord, for loving me and all Your creation. Amen.

---

* "All Creatures of Our God and King," words by Francis of Assisi, 1225; trans. William H. Draper, 1925; music *Geistliche Kirchengesänge*, 1623; arr. Ralph Vaughan Williams, 1906, public domain.

DAY 18

Saint Francis of Assisi

ᨒ

Submission and Self-Denial

Then he called the crowd to him along with his disciples and said: "Whoever wants to be my disciple must deny themselves and take up their cross and follow me. For whoever wants to save their life will lose it, but whoever loses their life for me and for the gospel will save it." (Mark 8:34–35)

Two words at the center of the nature of the Christian life that give us a lot of difficulty in thought and practice are *submission* and *self-denial*. Not only are these the most difficult of all the disciplines for spiritual growth, but they may also be the most dangerous. When misunderstood and abused, they can play havoc in our lives.

This is a problem as we seek to appropriate the message of Saint Francis. He talked and wrote most about simplicity, poverty, humility, and obedience. Saints alive! He concluded:

There is absolutely no man in the whole world who can possess one among you [simplicity, poverty, humility, or obedience] unless he first die. He who possesses one and does not offend the others, possesses all; and he who offends one, possesses none and offends all; and every one of them confounds vices and sins.*

He contended that these should be the characteristics of a *true* Jesus follower, and he was constantly celebrating them:

Pure holy simplicity confounds all the wisdom of this world and the wisdom of the flesh. Holy poverty confounds cupidity and avarice and the cares of this world. Holy humility confounds pride and all the men of this world and all things that are in the world. Holy charity confounds all diabolical and fleshly temptations and all fleshly fears.†

Following that celebration of a true Christian character, he adds the word that gives us the most trouble: "Holy obedience confounds all bodily and fleshly desires and keeps the body mortified to the obedience of the spirit."‡

History contains some horrible examples, especially in the monastic movement of the church, of persons practicing the physical

---

* J. Minton Batten, arr. and ed., *Selections from the Writings of St. Francis of Assisi* (Nashville, TN: The Upper Room, 1952), 14.

† Batten, *Writings of St. Francis of Assisi*, 14.

‡ Batten, *Writings of St. Francis of Assisi*, 14.

mortification of the body to develop the discipline of submission and self-denial. They were seeking to be faithful to Peter's call to offer "spiritual sacrifices acceptable to God through Jesus Christ" (1 Peter 2:5). They have connected the call to repent with the practice of *penance,* somehow paying for our sins. The distorted notion has been that a person can pay for the sins of the body by causing the body to suffer. Just as distorted is the notion that we should mortify the body to "bring it into subjection" to the Spirit—a misinterpretation of 1 Corinthians 9:27 (NKJV).

At times, Saint Francis's teaching seems to be extreme in this matter. However, if we pay attention to his central message, we find that giving our bodies is useless if we have not yet given ourselves.

And let us hate our body with its vices and sins, because by living carnally it wishes to deprive us of the love our Lord Jesus Christ and eternal life, and to lose itself with all else in hell; for we by our own fault are corrupt, miserable, and averse to good, but prompt and willing to evil; because, as the Lord says in the Gospel: from the heart of men proceed and come evil thoughts, adulteries, fornications, murders, thefts, covetousness, wickedness, deceit, lasciviousness, an evil eye, false testimonies, blasphemy, foolishness. All these evils come from within, from the heart of man, and these are what defile a man. But now, after having renounced the world, we have nothing else to do but to be solicitous, to follow the will of God, and to please Him.

And let us be much on our guard against the malice and cunning of Satan, who desires that man should not give his heart and mind to the Lord God, and who going about seeks to seduce the heart of man under pretext of some reward or benefit, to smolder the words and precepts of the Lord from memory, and who wishes to blind the heart of man by worldly business and cares.*

Only in surrendering and submitting ourselves to God, and in our earnest desire to know and follow His will, does our submission and self-denial have meaning. Our acts of self-sacrifice and surrender mean nothing if they are efforts to prove our merit or earn salvation.

REFLECTIVE MOMENT: How are you practicing submission and self-denial? What are you finding most difficult and most meaningful?

PRAYER: Lord Jesus, make me more committed, but relaxed in my efforts at submission and self-denial. Amen.

---

* Batten, *Writings of St. Francis of Assisi*, 21.

DAY 19
Thomas à Kempis

∽

Following Christ

When Jesus spoke again to the people, he said, "I am the light of the world. Whoever follows me will never walk in darkness, but will have the light of life." (John 8:12)

I n his introduction to *The Imitation of Christ*, Douglas Steere wrote:

There is something startling about the title of the *Imitation of Christ*. Who would have the presumption to think that his life could imitate that of Jesus Christ? And yet for over 500 years the invitation contained in that title has helped to make this little book, outside the Bible, the favorite devotional book of Christians of all faith and nationalities and persuasions.[*]

---

* Thomas à Kempis, *The Imitation of Christ*, Living Selections from the Great Devotional Classics, arr. and ed. Douglas V. Steere (Nashville, TN: The Upper Room, 1950), 5.

The first entry in the "Selections" edition is good confirmation for why Thomas à Kempis's *The Imitation of Christ* is so popular and powerful:

> "He that followeth me walketh not in darkness," saith the Lord. These are the words of Christ, by which we are taught to imitate his life and manners, if we would be truly enlightened, and be delivered from all blindness of heart. Let therefore our chief endeavor be to meditate upon the life of Christ. . . . Whosoever would fully and feelingly understand the words of Christ must endeavor to conform his life wholly to the life of Christ. . . . Surely great words do not make a man holy and just; but a virtuous life maketh him dear to God.
>
> Some have me in their mouths, but little in their hearts.
>
> Thou hast good cause to be ashamed in looking upon the life of Jesus Christ, seeing thou hast not as yet endeavored to conform thyself more unto him, though thou hast been a long time in the way of God.[*]

In one of his books, Karl Heim writes prophetically: "What Jesus wants is not admirers, but disciples.

Pay attention to the different ways Jesus calls us, beginning with our theme text:

---

* Kempis, *Imitation of Christ*, 13.

"I am the light of the world. Whoever follows me will never walk in darkness, but will have the light of life." (John 8:12)

"Whoever wants to be my disciple must deny themselves and take up their cross and follow me." (Matt. 16:24)

"And whoever does not carry their cross and follow me cannot be my disciple." (Luke 14:27)

"Whoever wants to be my disciple must deny themselves and take up their cross daily and follow me." (Luke 9:23)

"By this everyone will know that you are my disciples, if you love one another." (John 13:35)

Disciple is the common word in these calls. And what is a disciple? A learner and a follower. Underscore the fact that the designation does not suggest a religious genius. If it did, we might be able to better deal with it. Saints alive! As we study the saints we discover that a disciple, or an apostle, is just a name for a human being released from the love of self and enslaved by the love of God.

Thus, *The Imitation of Christ* challenges us from the very beginning:

Thou hast good cause to be ashamed in looking upon the life of Jesus Christ, seeing thou hast not as yet endeavored to conform thyself more unto him, though thou hast been a long time in the way of God.

For a small income a long journey is undertaken; for ever-lasting life many will scarce once lift a foot from the ground.[*]

I have begun, I may not go back, neither is it fit to leave that which I have undertaken. Courage then, brethren, let us go forward together. Jesus will be with us. . . He will be our helper who is also our guide and forerunner.[†]

———————————— ⌒ ————————————

REFLECTIVE MOMENT: Examine your life in this way: Where are you on the move from being an admirer to being a disciple?

PRAYER: O Lord Jesus, I know Your way is narrow. Even though following You may become narrow and rough, give me persistence and strength to carry on. Amen.

---

[*] Kempis, *Imitation of Christ*, 13.
[†] Kempis, *Imitation of Christ*, 14.

DAY 20
Thomas à Kempis

⌒

Daily Self-Examination

Have mercy on me, O God, according to thy steadfast love;
according to thy abundant mercy blot out my transgressions.
Wash me thoroughly from my iniquity,
    and cleanse me from my sin!

For I know my transgressions,
    and my sin is ever before me.
Against thee, thee only, have I sinned
    and done that which is evil in thy sight,
so that thou art justified in thy sentence
    and blameless in thy judgment. (Ps. 51:1–4 RSV)

None of us are exempt from the possibility of moral and spiritual failure. A big part of history is the story of the fall of great men. Think of King David, "a man after [God's] own heart" (1 Sam. 13:14). Scripture calls him the hero of Israel, the singer of

God's songs of praise and trust and confidence. But as we see in the beginning verses of Psalm 51, he miserably fails.

None of us are exempt. Our task as Christians is to be vigilant in staying alive to the ongoing presence and power of Christ.

The Imitation of Christ warned us:

> There is no worse enemy, nor one more troublesome to the soul, than thou art to thyself, if thou be not in harmony with the Spirit. . . .
>
> So much inclined to outward things, so negligent in things inward and spiritual: So prone to laughter and unbridled mirth, so indisposed to tears and compunction: So prompt to ease and pleasures of the flesh, so dull to strictness of life and zeal: So curious to hear news and to see beautiful sights, so slack to embrace what is humble and low: So covetous of abundance, so niggardly in giving, so fast in keeping: So inconsiderate in speech, so reluctant to keep silence: So uncomposed in manners, so fretful in action: So eager about food, so deaf to the word of God . . . *

He continues with that litany, concluding: "Make thou a firm resolution always to be amending thy life, and to be endeavoring always after a farther progress in holiness."†

---

* Thomas à Kempis, *The Imitation of Christ*, arr. and ed. Douglas V. Steere (Nashville, TN: The Upper Room, 1950), 16–17.
† Kempis, *Imitation of Christ*, 17.

Following Christ, seeking to imitate Him, is everyday business. William Law, to whom we gave attention on days 4 through 6, put it simply and so clearly: "If we are to follow Christ, it must be our common way of spending every day."

For most of us, outright betrayal in our Christian walk is probably not a part of our experience—but denial is. Hardly a day passes for most of us when we do not deny Christ in one way or another.

Peter could tell us about that. He loved Jesus. He wanted to be faithful, but the pressure was too great. There, in the courtyard, when the heat was on, and the Galilean woman recognized the accent that marked him as a possible follower of Jesus, she confronted him. But Peter denied that he knew Jesus; in fact, he repeated that denial three times. That's when the rooster crowed, and that's when a bomb went off in Peter's mind. Jesus had told him this was going to happen (Matt. 26:69–75; Mark 14:66–72; Luke 22:54–62; John 18:15–17, 25–27).

That kind of dramatic betrayal and denial is probably not a part of our experience—but hardly a day passes, for most of us, when we do not deny in one way or another. In its most common expression, denial comes in our failure to daily live out our discipleship, paying attention to our attitudes, our language, our sensitivity to others, questioning how we are expressing values.

We must make daily examination a regular practice, asking ourselves questions like these at the close of the day: When did I fail in relationship to others—to love, to care, to understand, to listen, to support? Did I stand by when someone maligned the character of another? Did I fail to lend my moral weight to a cause of righteousness? We might also give some time to reflecting on when and how we felt closest to Christ. When did we have the opportunity to share Christ, to witness, but failed to do so?

The Imitation of Christ warns and guides us:

> Know that the old enemy doth strive by all means to hinder thy desire to good, and to divert thee from all religious exercises. . . . Many evil thoughts does he suggest to thee, that so he may cause a wearisomeness and horror in thee, to call thee back from prayer and holy reading. . . . Trust him not, nor heed him although he should often set snares of deceit to entrap thee. . . .
>
> No man doth safely appear abroad, but he who can abide at home. No man doth safely speak but he that is glad to hold his peace. . . . No man doth safely rule, but he that hath learned gladly to obey.
>
> Seek a convenient time of leisure for thyself, and meditate often upon God's loving kindness.
>
> If thou desirest true contrition of heart, enter into thy secret chamber, and shut out the tumults of the world; as it is written, "Commune with your own heart, and in your chamber, and be still."

The more thou visitest thy chamber, the more thou wilt enjoy it; the less thou comest thereunto, the more thou wilt loathe it.*

Daily self-examination is an essential discipline, and we must make it a habit.

REFLECTIVE MOMENT: In what ways, and how often, do you practice self-examination?

PRAYER: Jesus, refresh my longing for intimate fellowship with You, and burn through my coldness with the fire of Your love. Amen.

---

* Kempis, *Imitation of Christ*, 23–24.

DAY 21
Thomas à Kempis

‹‒›

Living with Others

Those who belong to Christ Jesus have crucified the flesh with its passions and desires. Since we live by the Spirit, let us keep in step with the Spirit. Let us not become conceited, provoking and envying each other. (Gal. 5:24–26)

The Christian walk is a shared journey. We do not walk alone; others walk with us. In his letters to different churches, Paul gives guidance for our journey together. The notion of interrelatedness and interdependence is laced throughout his letters. If one member suffers, all suffer together; if one member is honored, all rejoice together (1 Cor. 12:26). "We who are strong ought to bear with the failings of the weak" (Rom. 15:1).

The new life into which we have been born through Christ is a shared life. The Greek word used to describe this shared life of the people of God was *koinonia*. Our best word for it in English is *fellowship*, but the word is far too limited to encompass the meaning of it. Because we belong to Christ, we belong to each other. In koinonia we are bound to each other, to Christ, and to God. Our life is a shared life.

The Imitation of Christ counsels about this in different ways. One way to which most of us need to pay attention is "bearing with the defects . . . of others."

> Endeavor to be patient in bearing with the defects and infirmities of others, of what sort soever they be: for that thyself also hast many failings which must be borne with by others. If thou canst not make thyself such an one as thou wouldst, how canst thou expect to have another in all things to thy liking? We would willing have others perfect, and yet we amend not our own faults. We will have others severely corrected, and will not be corrected ourselves. The large liberty of others displeaseth us; and yet we will not have our own desires denied us. We will have others kept under by strict laws; but in no sort will ourselves be restrained. And thus it appeareth, how seldom we weigh our neighbor in the same balance with ourselves.*

---

* Thomas à Kempis, *The Imitation of Christ*, arr. and ed. Douglas V. Steere (Nashville, TN: The Upper Room, 1950), 27.

We need to ask ourselves why it is that we find it so easy to judge and condemn, so difficult to love and forgive, when we know that is the only way of redemption.

We also need to be more honest about how we might be rightly under judgment ourselves. A test might come in answering questions like these:

- Have you been aware of some jealousy which prevented you from celebrating the success of someone you know, maybe even a loved one?
- Have you refused the word of another as truth because you still harbor the memory of a lie he told you?
- Have you participated in keeping alive a morsel of destructive gossip? Could it be that keeping alive that destructive word is an effort on your part to pay back that person for something they did to you? Or maybe you have an unrecognized desire to hurt someone else because you have been hurt?
- Have you secretly delighted in the misfortune of another? Maybe *delighted* is too strong a word; have you had that smiling feeling while the person got what you thought he or she deserved?

The Imitation of Christ counsels us:

Be careful also to avoid with great diligence those things in thyself which do commonly displease thee in others.

If there is any good in thee, believe that there is much more in others, that so thou mayest preserve humility. It

hurteth you not to submit to all men: but it hurteth thee
most of all to prefer thyself even to one.

If thy heart were sincere and upright, then every creature would be unto thee a living mirror, and a book of
holy doctrine.*

Again, as Christians, ours is a shared life. On this issue of not
judging, *The Imitation of Christ* builds on Paul's further call to
koinonia: "Each one should test their own actions. Then they can
take pride in themselves alone, without comparing themselves to
someone else" (Gal. 6:4). So *The Imitation of Christ* counsels about
hearing criticism:

My son, stand steadily, and put thy trust in me; for what are
words, but words? They fly through the air, but hurt not the
rock. If thou be guilty, see that thou be willing to amend
thyself; if conscience reproach thee not, resolve to suffer
willingly for God's sake. It is but a small matter to suffer
sometimes a few words, if thou hast not yet the courage to
endure hard stripes. And why do such small things go to thy
heart, but because thou are yet carnal, and regardest men
more than thou oughtest? For because thou art afraid to be
despised, therefore thou art not willing to be reproved for
thy faults, but seekest the shelter of excuses. But look better

* Kempis, *Imitation of Christ*, 28.

into thyself and thou shalt acknowledge that the world is yet alive in thee, and a vain desire to please men. . . .

Let not thy peace depend on the tongues of men; for, whether they judge well of thee or ill, thou art not on that account other than thyself. Where are true peace and true glory? Are they not in me?*

REFLECTIVE MOMENT: Do you assess and measure yourself by comparing yourself to others?

PRAYER: Loving Father, condition me to let Your grace alone be how I measure myself, and how I think and judge others. Amen.

---

* Kempis, *Imitation of Christ*, 29–30.

DAY 22
Søren Kierkegaard

~

The Lowly Jesus

This is what the LORD says:

> "Stand at the crossroads and look;
>   ask for the ancient paths,
> ask where the good way is, and walk in it,
>   and you will find rest for your souls." (Jer. 6:16)

"Come to me, all you who are weary and burdened, and I will give you rest. Take my yoke upon you and learn from me, for I am gentle and humble in heart, and you will find rest for your souls. For my yoke is easy and my burden is light." (Matt. 11:28–30)

O f all the saints we have called upon thus far, Søren Kierkegaard, whose counsel we begin to consider today, is perhaps the most unique in personality. From his own writing, we discover he was a very troubled soul: "I have been from childhood on in the grip of an overpowering melancholy, my sole joy being, as far as I can remember, that nobody could discover how unhappy I felt myself to be."*

He was born May 5, 1813, the youngest child of a large family. Comfort, gloominess, and strict loyalty to religion and the church pervaded his environment.

An outsider to the Christian faith would be puzzled that such a person's teaching would be considered, and more mystified that such a person would witness to astounding faith in God. Though we know his testimony is not typical, we Christians know the faith he claimed is available to all.

In his period of great creativity and productivity (1843–1846), he wrote a book every three months, besides his journal. He wrote twelve hours a day, testifying: "I have literally lived with God as one lives with a Father. Amen. I rise up in the morning and give thanks to God. Then it is again work. At a set time in the evening I break off and again give thanks to God. Then I sleep. Thus do I live."†

It is helpful to know that the thoughts of Kierkegaard reflect his reaction against self-reliance, feeling that is man's worst sin. "The smugness of the State Church was illustrative of this self-assurance. Man needs to despair of his inadequacy and be brought face to face

---

* Thomas S. Kepler, arr. and ed., *Selections from the Writings of Søren Kierkegaard* (Nashville, TN: The Upper Room, 1952), 4–5.
† Kepler, *Writings of Søren Kierkegaard*, 6.

with God; only when man accepts his own spiritual bankruptcy can he be brought before God."*

This conviction shaped the way he visualized and saw Jesus. The first entry in *Selections from the Writings of Søren Kierkegaard* reflects this.

> Come hither unto me, all ye that labor and are heavy laden, I will give you rest. . . . Who is the Inviter? Jesus Christ. Which Jesus Christ? The Jesus Christ who sits in glory at the right hand of the Father? No. From the seat of His glory He has not spoken one word. Therefore it is Jesus Christ in His humiliation, in the state of humiliation, who spoke these words.†

When I read this word, and began reflection on Kierkegaard, a gospel hymn I have probably not heard in forty years came to mind:

There's not a Friend like the lowly Jesus.
No, not one! No, not one! . . .
No friend like Him is so high and holy.
No, not one! No, not one!
And yet no friend is so meek and lowly.
No, not one! No, not one! . . .
There's not an hour that He is not near us.
No, not one! No, not one!

---

* Kepler, *Writings of Søren Kierkegaard*, 7.
† Kepler, *Writings of Søren Kierkegaard*, 9.

No night so dark but His love can cheer us.

   No, not one! No, not one!*

I began hearing this hymn as a teenager in churches in rural Mississippi. It was a favorite of my parents and others like them who were poor and deprived in many ways. It was easy for them to identify with the lowly Jesus.

Kierkegaard wanted the smug members to know the nature of the one who extended the invitation, "Come to me" (Matt. 11:28). It was Jesus Christ, in His humiliation, who spoke these words.

Is then Jesus Christ not always the same? Yes, He is the same yesterday and today, the same that 1,800 years ago humbled Himself and took upon Him the form of a servant, the Jesus Christ who utter these words of invitation. In His coming again in glory He is again the same Jesus Christ, but this has not yet occurred.

   Is He, then, how now in glory? Yes indeed; . . . But it was in the state of humiliation He uttered these words: from the seat of His glory He has not uttered them. And about His coming again in glory nothing can be known; in the strictest sense, it can only be believed. But one cannot have become a Christian without having already come to Him, who is the sign of offence and the object of faith. . . . That he shall come

_____

* "No, Not One!," words by Johnson Oatman Jr., music by George C. Hugg, 1890, public domain.

again in glory is to be expected, but can be expected and believed by one who has attached himself and continues to hold fast to Him as He actually existed.*

Again, I think of the hymn. Not only is it Christ-centered, identifying Christ as "the lowly Jesus," but it also begins and concentrates on the qualities of Jesus as the Christian's constant companion, a friend who "will guide till the day is done." Verse 3 reminds us of the Lord's promise to never leave His followers: "There's not an hour that He is not near us. No, not one! No, not one!" Verse 4 speaks of Jesus's desire to help all who need Him: "Did ever a saint find this friend forsake him? No, not one! No, not one! Or sinner find that He would not take him? No, not one! No, not one!"†

REFLECTIVE MOMENT: In your everyday life, and in worship, what is your primary image of Jesus? Do you think much about "a friend like the lowly Jesus"?

PRAYER: Eternal God, our Father, increase in us the spirit of Him who took the form of a servant, humbled Himself, and became obedient unto death. Don't let us forget that he who humbles himself will be exalted. Amen.

---

* Kepler, *Writings of Søren Kierkegaard*, 9–10.
† "No, Not One!," Oatman and Hugg.

DAY 23
Søren Kierkegaard

⤶

A Place in God's Heart

Dear friends, let us love one another, for love comes from God. Everyone who loves has been born of God and knows God. Whoever does not love does not know God, because God is love. This is how God showed his love among us: He sent his one and only Son into the world that we might live through him. This is love: not that we loved God, but that he loved us and sent his Son as an atoning sacrifice for our sins. (1 John 4:7–10)

It is one of my central convictions. I can't guarantee that it is original with me; if it isn't, I don't know where it came from. There is a place in God's heart that only I can fill. Scripture verifies, and I believe this conviction is confirmed by the great devotional classics. Certainly Kierkegaard confirms, though in the unique way of using syllogism:

This is the syllogism. Love (true love, not self-love which loves the remarkable, the brilliant and consequently really loves itself) stands in inverse ratio to the greatness and excellence of the object. And so if I am of infinitely, infinitely little importance, if in my wretchedness I feel myself to be the most miserable of all: then it is eternally, eternally certain that God loves me.

Christ says: not a sparrow shall fall to earth unless it be at His will. Oh, I bid lower still, to God I am less than a sparrow—that God loves me becomes more certain still, the syllogism more solid still in its conclusion.

It might seem to the Emperor of Russia that God could overlook him. God has so much to attend to and the Emperor of Russia is so great. But not a sparrow—for God is love, and love is in inverse ratio to the greatness and excellence of the object.*

Saints alive! Our relationship to God is not only of value to us, but of value to God. Augustine said, "Thou hast made us for thyself, O God, and our hearts are restless until they rest in Thee." But here is the question: Could it be true that there is a place in God's heart that only you can fill, that only I can fill, that God is restless until we rest in Him?

---

* Thomas S. Kepler, arr. and ed., *Selections from the Writings of Søren Kierkegaard* (Nashville, TN: The Upper Room, 1952), 19–20.

That God is love and has a place in His heart that only you can fill is more than a thought. It's a truth verified in the most dramatic and convincing way: "For God so loved the world, that He gave His only begotten Son, that whoever believes in Him should not perish but have everlasting life" (John 3:16 NKJV).

Lay hold on what that means. God is forever restless until you come to Him. If we love someone, we need that someone to love us. So with God. He loves you, and needs you to love Him. He will not allow death to destroy you. If your sin forever separates you from Him, it will be your choice, not His. God has a place in His heart that only you can fill. With unquestioned confidence, Kierkegaard writes:

> You feel lost in the world in your suffering, no one cares for you, alas, and you conclude, neither does God care for me. You fool! you traducer, to speak thus of God. No, if there were anyone of whom it were literally true that he was of all the most neglected—he is the one whom God loves. Or if he were not quite the most neglected, if he still had a little human consolation—and were taken from him: in this very moment it would be more certain still that God loves him.*

---

* Kepler, *Writings of Søren Kierkegaard*, 20.

REFLECTIVE MOMENT: What changes in thought, attitude, and action do you have to make and/or claim if you really believe there is a place in God's heart that only you can fill?

PRAYER: Eternal God, that I am important to You, the Lord of heaven and earth, fills me with new confidence. May I ever be worthy of Your love. Amen.

DAY 24
Søren Kierkegaard

___

The Exclusive and Inclusive Christ

Jesus answered, "I am the way and the truth and the life. No one comes to the Father except through me." (John 14:6)

Saints alive! We can't be a human and not judge. Judgments are part of life. We can't get through a day without judging. Judging is part of how we discern one thing from another, how we know what we like and what we don't. It's how we determine what is real and not real in our lives.

Because that is so much a part of living, it makes life especially difficult when many of our friends consider intolerance to be the worst sin in our culture: "And guess who are the worst sinners, at least in the minds of many Americans? Evangelical Christians! One writer said, 'Christians are seen as the pit bulls of culture wars—small brains, big teeth, strong jaws, and no interest in compromise."* The issue of religious toleration gets worlds of attention.

Saints alive! Jesus asserted: "I am the way and the truth and the life. No one comes to the Father except through me" (John 14:6). And Kierkegaard made bold claims that Christianity is the absolute.

> With this invitation to all them "that labor and are heavy laden" Christianity did not come into the world . . . as an admiral example of the gentle art of consolation—but as *the absolute*. It is out of love God wills it so, but also it is God who wills it, and He wills what He will. He will not suffer Himself to be transformed by men and be a nice . . . human God: He will transform me, and that He wills out of love. He will have nothing to do with man's pert inquiry about why and why did Christianity come into the world: it is and shall be the absolute. Therefore everything men have hit upon relatively to explain the why and the wherefore is falsehood.†

Jesus's claim "I am the way and the truth and the life. No one comes to the Father except through me" is an exclusive statement. Peter made that claim of Jesus even more blatant when he said,

---

* Bill Bouknight, "Is Jesus the Only Way? (Matt. 22:1–14; John 14:5–6)," https://www.preaching.com/sermons/is-jesus-the-only-way-matt-221-14-john-145-6/.

† Thomas S. Kepler, arr. and ed., *Selections from the Writings of Søren Kierkegaard* (Nashville, TN: The Upper Room, 1952), 22–23, italics in original.

"Salvation is found in no one else, for there is no other name under heaven given to mankind by which we must be saved" (Acts 4:12).

Lots of Americans almost wallow in tolerance. They feel that as long as a person is sincere about his religious beliefs, it doesn't matter what he believes. Unconsciously perhaps, they are diminishing even the importance of religion.

From the perspective of his time, Kierkegaard asked:

> But what, then, is the use of Christianity? It is, then, merely a plague to us! Ah, yes, that too can be said: relatively understood, the absolute is the greatest plague. In all moments of laxness, sluggishness, dullness, when the sensuous nature of man predominates, Christianity seems madness, since it is incommensurable with any finite wherefore. What is the use of it, then? [Saints alive!] The answer is: Hold thy peace! It is the absolute! And so it must be represented, viz., in such a way as to make it appear madness in the eyes of the sensuous man. And hence it is true, so true . . . when the wise and prudent man in the situation of contemporaneousness condemns Christ by saying, "He is literally nothing"—most certainly true, for He is the absolute.*

Sure enough . . . Jesus's claim was exclusive when He claimed that He was the only way to God the Father. It was, however, motivated not by arrogance but by compassion. While His claim was exclusive,

---

* Kepler, *Writings of Søren Kierkegaard*, 23.

His offer was inclusive. What can be more inclusive than "God so loved the world that . . . whoever believes" may come (John 3:16)?

Kierkegaard concluded his counsel on Christianity being the absolute:

> Christianity came into the world as the absolute—not for consolation, humanly understood; on the contrary, it speaks again and again of the sufferings which a Christian must endure, or which a man must endure to become a Christian, sufferings he can well avoid merely by refraining from becoming a Christian.*

REFLECTIVE MOMENT: How do you present the exclusive claim of Jesus without being considered a bigot?

PRAYER: Loving Father, save me from compromise, from substituting tolerance for genuine love for those who need desperately to know Christ as the Way. Amen.

---

* Kepler, *Writings of Søren Kierkegaard*, 23–24.

Dietrich Bonhoeffer

~

Cheap and Costly Grace

Do you not know that your bodies are temples of the Holy Spirit, who is in you, whom you have received from God? You are not your own; you were bought at a price. Therefore honor God with your bodies. (1 Cor. 6:19–20)

On that April morning in Flossenburg, Germany, when the Nazi Gestapo hanged Dietrich Bonhoeffer, violence once again proved that the human spirit is not only indestructible but that Christian man, under the witness of Jesus Christ, transcends all earthly powers, no matter how devastatingly terrible such powers may appear at that time.*

With these words, *Selections from the Writings of Dietrich Bonhoeffer* was introduced.

---

* Orlo Strunk Jr., arr. and ed., *Selections from the Writings of Dietrich Bonhoeffer* (Nashville, TN: The Upper Room, 1967), 4.

In the years since his death, Bonhoeffer has become probably the most widely known modern Christian martyr. The contemporary history of the church of which he was a part is stained by its complicity with Nazism.

Bonhoeffer's letters and theological works still influence Christians throughout the world. He is the most contemporary in the Upper Room Great Devotional Classics series.

Bonhoeffer made popular a discussion of cheap and costly grace, and his word about that is the first entry in the selection of his writings:

> Cheap grace is the preaching of forgiveness without requiring repentance, baptism without church discipline. Communion without confession, absolution without personal confession. Cheap grace is grace without discipleship, grace without the cross, grace without Jesus Christ, living and incarnate.*

Bonhoeffer had come to America because of his opposition to Hitler and his conflict with his church which was identifying with the Nazi movement. During his time here, he taught at Union Seminary. He was shocked at liberal theologians challenging the orthodox faith. He was especially concerned about how this was shaping students and the church itself.

Of that experience he wrote:

---

* Strunk, *Writings of Dietrich Bonhoeffer*, 7.

There is no theology here. . . . They talk a blue streak without the slightest substantive foundation. . . . The students . . . are completely clueless with respect to what dogmatics is really about. They are unfamiliar with even the most basic of questions. They become intoxicated with liberal and humanistic phrases, laugh at the fundamentalists, and yet basically are not even up to their level.*

Saints alive! No wonder he wrote:

Costly grace is the gospel which must be *sought* again and again, the gift which must be *asked* for, the door at which a man must *knock.*

Such grace is *costly* because it calls us to follow, and it is *grace* because it calls us to follow *Jesus Christ.* It is costly because it costs a man his life, and it is grace because it gives a man the only true life. It is costly because it condemns sin, and grace because it justifies the sinner. Above all, it is *costly* because it cost God the life of his Son; "ye were bought at a price," and what has cost God much cannot be cheap to us. Above all, it is *grace* because God did not reckon his Son too dear a price to pay for our life, but delivered him up for us. Costly grace is the Incarnation of God.†

---

* Eric Metaxas, *Bonhoeffer: Pastor, Martyr, Prophet, Spy* (Nashville, TN: Thomas Nelson, 2010), 101.
† Strunk, *Writings of Dietrich Bonhoeffer,* 7, italics in original.

Even in this brief discussion of grace, he mentions some of the basic fundamentals of the faith: Jesus, the Incarnate Son of God; sin and the need of redemption which comes only through justification that comes through faith in Jesus Christ; the cross, the cost of redemption. He felt these foundational dimensions of the gospel were being ignored, even trivialized, and thus threatened.

> Costly grace is the sanctuary of God; it has to be protected from the world, and not thrown to the dogs. It is therefore the living word, the Word of God, which he speaks as it pleases him. Costly grace confronts us as a gracious call to follow Jesus, it comes as a word of forgiveness to the broken spirit and the contrite heart. Grace is costly because it compels a man to submit to the yoke of Christ and follow him; it is grace because Jesus says: "My yoke is easy and my burden is light."*

REFLECTIVE MOMENT: Consider how grace has worked in your life through the years. In what ways has it been costly grace?

PRAYER: Forgive us for not staying aware that saving grace is costly. Guide us and give us strength to find the grace to follow You more closely. Amen.

---

* Strunk, *Writings of Dietrich Bonhoeffer*, 7–8.

DAY 26
Dietrich Bonhoeffer

~

Our Distinctive Identification

For it has been granted to you on behalf of Christ not only to believe in him, but also to suffer for him, since you are going through the same struggle you saw I had, and now hear that I still have. (Phil. 1:29–30)

A popular monk in the Middle Ages announced that in the cathedral that evening he would preach a sermon on the love of God. The people gathered and stood in silence waiting for the service while the sunlight streamed through the beautiful windows. When the last glint of color had faded from the windows, the old monk took a candle from the altar. Walking to the life-size figure of Christ on the cross, he held the light beneath the wounds of the feet, then His hands, then His side. Still without a word, he let the light shine on the thorn-crowned brow.

That was his sermon. The people stood in silence and wept. They knew they were at the center of mystery beyond their knowing, that they were looking at the love of God, the image of the invisible God, giving Himself for us—a love so deep, so inclusive, so expansive, so powerful, so complete that the mind could not comprehend or measure it, or words express it.

Yet, we have to consider it, talk about it, reflect on it, seek to live lives responsive to it.

In his epistle to the Philippians, Paul expresses the radical notion that believing and suffering go together. This is not something to shun, but something to celebrate. Most translations use the word *privilege* in the verse. We're given the privilege, not merely of believing in Christ, but also of suffering for his cause. The cross is at the center of the Christian life—not just Golgotha's cross, though that is our salvation—but the cross as a way of life. Prior to Golgotha, Jesus suffered persecution, rejection, hostility, and misunderstanding. He promised His followers nothing less in their ministry in His name.

Bonhoeffer speaks eloquently and convincingly about that:

The cross means sharing the suffering of Christ to the last and to the fullest. Only a man thus totally committed in discipleship can experience the meaning of the cross. The cross is there, right from the beginning, he has only to pick it up; there is no need for him to go out and look for a cross for himself, no need for him deliberately to run after suffering.*

---

* Orlo Strunk Jr., arr. and ed., *Selections from the Writings of Dietrich Bonhoeffer* (Nashville, TN: The Upper Room, 1967), 13.

Saints alive! The cross is our identity as Christians! It is not alone our source of salvation; it is the sign and fruit of our exclusive allegiance to Jesus Christ.

If our Christianity has ceased to be serious about discipleship, if we have watered down the gospel into emotional uplift which makes no costly demands and which fails to distinguish between natural and Christian existence, then we cannot help regarding the cross as an ordinary everyday calamity, as one of the trials and tribulations of life.

Earlier than in the passage previously quoted, Paul gave his personal testimony, reflecting the cross at the center of his life. "I eagerly expect and hope that I will in no way be ashamed, but will have sufficient courage so that now as always Christ will be exalted in my body, whether by life or by death" (Phil. 1:20).

The identity of the cross is to be strong and recognizable; *in my body,* Paul says. Bonhoeffer concurs heartily with Paul.

> To endure the cross is not a tragedy; it is the suffering which is the fruit of an exclusive allegiance to Jesus Christ. When it comes, it is not an accident, but a necessity. It is not the sort of suffering which is inseparable from the mortal life, but the suffering which is an essential part of the specifically Christian life.*

> Jesus says that every Christian has his own cross waiting for him, a cross destined and appointed by God. Each must

---

* Strunk, *Writings of Dietrich Bonhoeffer,* 12.

endure his allotted share of suffering and rejection. But each has a different share: some God deems worthy of the highest form of suffering, and gives them the grace of martyrdom, while other He does not allow to be tempted above that they are able to bear. But it is the one and the same cross in every case.[*]

The gospel is communicated through the person, and it will not shine to its most glorious brightness until the person bears the identity of the cross.

REFLECTIVE MOMENT: Has there been a cross for you "there, right from the beginning"? If not, have you experienced bearing a cross now and then? Are you open to the cross being your identity as a Christian?

PRAYER: Loving Lord, I want to communicate the gospel through my person, who I am. Strengthen me to bear my present cross, and/or any cross that may come my way. Amen.

---

[*] Strunk, *Writings of Dietrich Bonhoeffer*, 13.

DAY 27
Dietrich Bonhoeffer

~

Silence and Speaking

Silver and gold have I none; but such as I have give I thee.
(Acts 3:6 KJV)

The gospel puts us all on common ground. God requires of each of us such as we have. Peter and John were on the way to worship, when confronted by a beggar. Peter responded to him, "Silver and gold have I none; but such as I have give I thee."

I have long been convinced that we Christians need to pay more attention to both silence and speaking; both are the "such as I have" with the time and attention we give to others.

Bonhoeffer thought both silence and speaking were part of our discipleship, and he wrote about them in his book *The Cost of Discipleship*. Both are included in *Selections from the Writings of Dietrich Bonhoeffer*: "Silence is nothing else but waiting for God's Word with a blessing. But everybody knows that this is something that needs to be practiced and learned, in these days when talkativeness prevails."*

I talk far more than I listen. Not listening, I miss a great opportunity. When I listen, I am saying to the person, "You matter; I value you, I will hear what you have to say." Such as I have, I am giving, and that is blessing another.

Bonhoeffer spoke about listening when we read Scripture:

Consecutive reading of biblical books forces everyone who wants to hear to put himself, or to allow himself to be found, where God has acted once and for all for the salvation of men. . . . Forgetting and losing ourselves, we, too, pass through the Red Sea, through the desert, across the Jordan into the promised land. With Israel we fall into doubt and unbelief and through punishment and repentance experience again God's help and faithfulness. All this is not mere reverie but holy, godly reality. We are torn out of our own existence and set down in the midst of the holy history of God on earth. There God dealt with us, and there He still deals with us, our needs and our sins, in judgment and grace. It is not that God is the spectator and sharer of our present life, howsoever important that is; but rather that we are the reverent listeners and participants in God's action

---

* Orlo Strunk Jr., arr. and ed., *Selections from the Writings of Dietrich Bonhoeffer* (Nashville, TN: The Upper Room, 1967), 17.

in the sacred story, the history of the Christ on earth. And only in so far as we are *there*, is God with us today.[*]

One of our most important spiritual disciplines is what John Wesley designated "Christian conferencing." This discipline is practiced in small groups, gathered for the specific purpose of sharing fellowship with the purpose of upbuilding each other, sharing of need, and ministering and praying for one another. It is a setting where explicit Christian conversation takes place. The practice we get in such a group enables us to speak as Christians in everyday life, where, according to Bonhoeffer, is much needed.

> Where Christians live together the time must inevitably come when in some crisis one person will have to declare God's Word and will to another. It is inconceivable that the things that are of utmost importance to each individual should not be spoken to one another. It is unchristian consciously to deprive another of the one decisive service we can render to him. If we cannot bring ourselves to utter it, we shall have to ask ourselves whether we are not still seeing our brother garbed in his human dignity which we are afraid to touch, and thus forgetting the most important thing, that he, too, no matter how highly placed or distinguished he may be, is still a man like us, a sinner in crying

---

[*] Strunk, *Writings of Dietrich Bonhoeffer*, 14–15, italics in original.

need of God's grace. He has the same great necessities that we have, and needs help, encouragement, and forgiveness as we do. . . .

Why should we be afraid of one another, since both of us have only God to fear? Why should we think that our brother would not understand us, when we understood very well what was meant when somebody spoke God's comfort or God's admonition to us, perhaps in words that were halting and unskilled? Or do we really think there is a single person in this world who does not need either encouragement or admonition? Why, then, has God bestowed Christian brotherhood upon us?*

"Such as I have give I thee." All of us have time, and God requires each of us to give such as we have in silence and speaking.

REFLECTIVE MOMENT: Recall some instances and examine the way you have listened and spoken when with others. Did you give "such as [you] have"?

PRAYER: Ever speaking and listening, Lord, give me the wisdom to know when to speak and a willingness to be silent. Give me words, and a willingness to speak them as would serve You well. Amen.

---

* Strunk, *Writings of Dietrich Bonhoeffer*, 17–18.

John Knox

～⌒～

What Is Your Job?

"Come to me, all you who are weary and burdened, and I will give you rest. Take my yoke upon you and learn from me, for I am gentle and humble in heart, and you will find rest for your souls. For my yoke is easy and my burden is light." (Matt. 11:28–30)

When we meet someone we haven't known, we don't get far in the conversation before we ask: "And what is your job?" Many times we ask the same question another way: "And what do you do?" Hardly ever, but now and then we may ask: "And what is your vocation?"

We have not thought about it much, if at all, but *job* and *vocation* are not necessarily the same. Most of us have a job; all of us have a vocation!

Scripture and many of the saints talked about this. Referring explicitly to the notion of vocation, John Knox wrote:

There two kinds of vocation. One is immediately from God,
as the prophets and apostles were called to be preachers
without the authority of man. Another is mediated, as when
one man called another, as Paul called Timothy and Titus to
be bishops.*

But then he said:

There is a general vocation, by which all the chosen are
called to a Christian profession, having one Lord, one faith,
one baptism. In this vocation there is no distinction between
persons, but all are equally loved by God, because we are
all sons of the Father, and all bought with one price, all
servants of one Lord, all guided by one Spirit, all tending to
one end, and all shall participate in one heritage, that is, the
life eternal by Jesus Christ, by whom we are all made priests
and kings.†

While we may spend forty hours a week in our job, what God has
called us to do—our vocation—may involve only a few hours a week.
God has called us to do a particular vocation which may have little
or no connection with what we do as our job.

Almost every Sunday, I attend the Lamplighters Sunday school
class at our church in Memphis. The fellowship and mutual caring

---

* Norman Victor Hope, arr. and ed., *Selections from the Writings of John
Knox* (Nashville, TN: The Upper Room, 1957), 7.
† Hope, *Writings of John Knox*, 7–8.

in that class is a model for the whole church. What has shaped and continues to inspire that class is the teacher. For more than forty years, Dr. Jim Eoff has faithfully prepared and taught the Bible to a group that started out as the "young married class," but now has people most of who are over sixty.

Until he retired a few years ago, Jim's job was as a pharmacist and a professor, but his vocation has been teaching the Lamplighters.

Like Jim, our specific response to Christ's call may be teaching Sunday school, volunteering at a hospital, visiting the sick, doing evangelistic visitation, or working with young people.

REFLECTIVE MOMENT: What is your vocation? Are you giving it the time and attention needed?

PRAYER: Lord, continue to give me the will to be faithful, and not grow weary in well-doing. Amen.

DAY 29
John Knox

~

Me, a Saint?

For this reason, since the day we heard about you, we have not stopped praying for you. We continually ask God to fill you with the knowledge of his will through all the wisdom and understanding that the Spirit gives, so that you may live a life worthy of the Lord and please him in every way: bearing fruit in every good work, growing in the knowledge of God, being strengthened with all power according to his glorious might so that you may have great endurance and patience, and giving joyful thanks to the Father, who has qualified you to share in the inheritance of his holy people in the kingdom of light. For he has rescued us from the dominion of darkness and brought us into the kingdom of the Son he loves, in whom we have redemption, the forgiveness of sins. (Col. 1:9–14)

Paul begins his letter to the Colossians with this greeting: "To the saints and faithful brothers [and sisters] in Christ in Colossae" (v. 2 ESV). Later he reminds them that the Father "has qualified you to share in the inheritance of his holy people in the kingdom of light" (v. 12).

Saints. What does that image conjure in your mind? Stained glass? A well-lighted painting in a museum, like El Greco's *Saint Jerome*, which I saw at the Metropolitan in New York a few years ago? Paul uses the word *saint* in his greeting as a sublime synonym for Christians: "To the saints and faithful brethren in Christ" (v. 2 NKJV).

The word *saint* is drenched with meaning. It is a Greek word, *hagios*, which means "a holy person." *Holy* designates what belongs to God, and here in this text, it's a term that identifies a person who is set apart. God had called these people, and offered them His grace. They had received that grace, and God's love and forgiveness had made them new persons.

Our vocation is to be saints. Yesterday we focused on vocation, considering the difference between our job or profession and our vocation. Sometimes they are the same, but if your vocation and your profession are not the same, you are in good company. Perhaps the most well-known person in our Christian history was Paul, who wrote our text and a huge part of the New Testament. His vocation was evangelism and church planting, but he often had to exercise his job as a tent maker.

To make the case more dramatically, consider the Old Testament prophet Amos. We may know and connect him with the challenging prophetic word, "Let justice run down like water, and righteousness like a mighty stream" (Amos 5:24 NKJV), yet we may have never heard or read his testimony: "I was neither a prophet nor the son of a prophet, but I was a shepherd, and I also took care of sycamore-fig trees. But the LORD took me from tending the flock and said to me, 'Go, prophesy to my people Israel.' Now then, hear the word of the LORD" (Amos 7:14–16).

Interestingly, not only Amos and Paul, but a great host of biblical people had a job and a vocation.

Most of us can fulfill our vocation while doing our job. Teaching is our job, but we fulfill our vocation by calling forth the gifts of our students and motivating them to learn. Practicing law is our profession; our vocation in our job is to see that there is equal justice under the law. As doctors and nurses, our profession is practicing medicine; healing is our vocation. For mothers and fathers who stay at home and care for families, homemaking is a job, but nurturing the people in our family is a very significant vocation.

Most of us have a job; all of us have a vocation. John Knox challenges us to see that vocation in its richness:

> It becomes us to consider the excellence of our vocation, and the due and willing obedience we as children ought to render to so loving and gracious a Father, who of His free grace has called us from the darkness of error, and from bondage to Satan, to the bright knowledge of His glory and to the glorious liberty of His saints, whose kingdom, glory

and joy, He has appointed most assuredly and triumphantly with Christ Jesus His only beloved . . .*

———————————— ⌒ ————————————

REFLECTIVE MOMENT: Recall a recent occurrence of experiencing your vocation while doing your job.

PRAYER: Lord, give me guidance to perceive opportunities and practice my vocation while doing my job. Amen.

---

* Norman Victor Hope, arr. and ed., *Selections from the Writings of John Knox* (Nashville, TN: The Upper Room, 1957), 8.

DAY 30
John Knox

⁓

The Temptation of Jesus

The Spirit immediately drove him out into the wilderness. And he was in the wilderness forty days, tempted by Satan; and he was with the wild beasts; and the angels ministered to him. (Mark 1:12–13 RSV)

A man went to his counselor about a personal problem, saying, "I have a real struggle. I feel like I'm violating my conscience. I'm not being completely honest with myself. I'm living a broken life."

The counselor said to him, "Well, would you like to see me about strengthening your will power?"

The man thought for a moment and replied, "No, what I would like to talk to you about is weakening my conscience."

Does that man reflect our age? We are not so much interested in developing our conscience as we are in finding a way to live the way we wish without feeling guilty.

It's interesting and informing that a huge temptation experience came at the beginning of Jesus's ministry. When Jesus was
anointed by the Holy Spirit at His baptism in the river Jordan,
the gospel of Matthew says that He was "led by the Spirit into
the wilderness to be tempted by the devil" (Matt. 4:1). When we
examine Luke's account of the temptation, we find an intriguing
thought, as he says, "Jesus, full of the Holy Spirit, left the Jordan
and was led by the Spirit into the wilderness" (Luke 4:1). Later, in
verse 14, Luke says that "Jesus returned to Galilee in the power of
the Spirit." Note that when Jesus went into temptation, He went in
"full" of the Spirit. When he came out, it was "in the power of the
Spirit." In the life of Jesus, all that temptation could achieve was to
turn *fullness* into *power*.

John Knox imagines that Satan, by all ingenuity and craft, did:

> assail [Christ] to see what advantage he could have of
> Him; and Christ did not repel him (as by the power of His
> Godhead He might have) that he should not tempt Him, but
> permitted [Satan] to spend all his artillery, and received the
> assaults of his temptation in His own body, to the end that
> He might weaken and enfeeble the strength and tyrannous
> power of our adversary by His longsuffering. . . .*

---

* Norman Victor Hope, arr. and ed., *Selections from the Writings of John
Knox* (Nashville, TN: The Upper Room, 1957), 9–10.

We need to remember Jesus's experience when we are facing and wrestling with temptation. The word for *temptation* literally means "to put to the test" or "to go through." Jesus deliberately faced temptation as a man to show us that He has wrestled with the Enemy just as we have to. He proved by that experience that we are not helpless in the face of our most powerful temptation.

> What comfort the remembrance of these things ought to be in our hearts! Christ Jesus has fought the battle, He Himself has taken us under His care and protection; however violently the Devil may tempt us by temptations spiritual or physical, he is not able to pluck us out of the hand of the potent Son of God. To Him be all the glory, for his mercies most abundantly poured forth upon us!*

Even in temptation, God is working in us to bring us to full maturity in Christ. Temptation, testing, and trials—and how we endure them—may be used by God to grow us up into Christ.

REFLECTIVE MOMENT: Recall a particular temptation experience that inspired and provided spiritual growth. Are you developing the growth that came from that experience?

---

* Hope, *Writings of John Knox*, 10.

PRAYER: Lord, keep me mindful that all that happens to me may not be Your will, but You do have a will in everything that happens. Amen.

DAY 31
William Temple

〜

Sin Is Universal

See what great love the Father has lavished on us, that we should be called children of God! And that is what we are! The reason the world does not know us is that it did not know him. Dear friends, now we are children of God, and what we will be has not yet been made known. But we know that when Christ appears, we shall be like him, for we shall see him as he is. (1 John 3:1–2)

I like the cartoon character Brother Juniper, created by Father Justin McCarthy. He is such a human little monk; I hope there are a lot like him around our cloisters and monasteries. His humor and humanity prick holes in the balloons of superficial piety.

One cartoon pictures Brother Juniper with two little boys at the zoo; they are looking at a bird in a cage. The bird is an ugly crow-like creature, bedraggled, scrimpy in feathering, downcast-looking in every way, really ugly. "Bird of Paradise" is the label on the cage, and Brother Juniper says, "I don't think he quite made it."

That's our human situation. Speaking theologically, we call it *original sin*. All the saints I have lived with through their writing spoke of it in one way or another. William Temple labeled it "the least popular part of traditional Christianity: the doctrine of Original Sin."[*]

The Eden story is about original sin. In Brother Juniper's assessment of the "Bird of Paradise," we humans "didn't quite make it." We were created in God's image: whole. But we marred that image, perverted the wholeness, and now the struggle of our life is an inner and an outer one as we wander aimlessly in the land east of Eden. Temple talked about it this way:

> When we open our eyes as babies we see the world stretching out around us; we are in the middle of it; all proportions and perspectives in what we see are determined by the relation—distance, height, and so forth—of the various visible objects to ourselves. This will remain true of our bodily vision as long as we live. . . . So each of us takes his place at the centre of his own world. But I am not the centre of the world, or the standard of reference between good and bad; I am not, and God is. In other words, from the beginning I put myself in God's place. This is my original sin . . . I am in a state, from birth, in which I shall bring disaster upon myself and everyone affected by my conduct unless I can escape from it.[†]

---

[*] Sulon G. Ferree, arr. and ed., *Selections from the Writings of William Temple* (Nashville, TN: The Upper Room, 1968), 10.
[†] Ferree, *Writings of William Temple*, 10.

God has provided not only a way of redemption, but a way of recovering the broken image. Consider our beginning scripture; we are "called children of God." We actually are!

Because of who we are, conversion must be an ongoing, dynamic reality in our lives. When we are honest, most of us readily confess with Paul that there is a war going on within us (Rom. 7:19–23). For some of us, the inner conflict is a full-scale war. For others who have been on the way a long time and have cultivated more grace, it may be more like guerrilla warfare, with pockets of enemy forces holding out here and there, moving in for confrontations now and then.

With John Wesley, it is helpful to see original sin not as an obliteration of the image of God within us, but as a malignant disease that can be cured only by the powerful grace of God.

REFLECTIVE MOMENT: Ponder this thought: If sin is not *original,* it is certainly *universal.*

PRAYER: Lord Jesus, "Take away our bent to sinning, Alpha and Omega be; end of faith, as its beginning, set our hearts at liberty."* Amen.

---

* "Love Divine, All Loves Excelling," words by Charles Wesley, 1747; music by John Zundel, 1870, public domain.

DAY 32

William Temple

⌒

Repent! Get a New Mind

From that time Jesus began to preach and to say, "Repent, for the kingdom of heaven is at hand." (Matt. 4:17 NKJV)

I n *The Better Half* cartoon series, Bob Barnes pictured a husband and wife in their bedroom. The wife is combing her hair and "fixing" her face across the room from the husband, who is struggling to get out of bed. He sits wearily on the side of the bed, and moans, "I hope in my next reincarnation I come back as something easier to be than a human being."

When I read that I remembered the words of cartoonist and playwright Jules Feiffer: "Getting out of bed in the morning is an act of false confidence."*

---

* Jules Feiffer, *Hold Me!*, quoted by Clive Barnes in "Jules Feiffer's 'Hold Me!' Is a Look Back in Angst," *New York Times*, January 24, 1977,

Yesterday we began our consideration of sin, *original sin*. Whether we talk about this in terms of original sin or the universality of sin doesn't matter. The fact is that since Adam and Eve, sin has been a part of every human life. Paul gave expression to the anguishing conflict in his life, the constant war raging in his soul: "I want to do good, but I can't. I don't want to do evil, but I find myself doing it" (Rom. 7:15, 19, paraphrase mine). He continues: "Oh wretched man that I am! Who will deliver me from this body [doomed to] death?" (v. 24 NKJV).

There is something about our fallen nature that inclines us to commit individual acts of sin—that is words, thoughts, and deeds that go against God's nature and God's will for us. So there is sin, and there are sins. Sin is the universal tendency to oppose God's will, to order life on our own self-centered, self-directed terms, rather than God's terms. We may call this original sin, or the carnal nature, or the old man, or inherited sin, or moral depravity, or sinful nature. It is an inherent sinful disposition that inclines persons to sinful acts. Author Rita Mae Brown knew this when she said, "Lead me not into temptation; I can find the way myself.'" We are sinners.

---

https://www.nytimes.com/1977/01/24/archives/jules-feiffers-hold-me
-is-a-look-back-in-angst.html.
* Rita Mae Brown, quoted in sermon by Sam Candler, "The Ultimate Temptation Is to Doubt Who You Are," February 17, 2013, https://www.cathedralatl.org/sermons/the-ultimate-temptation-is-to-doubt
-who-you-are.

The most basic, fundamental response to this fact is repentance. After His temptation in the wilderness, Jesus began His ministry calling for a response to sin: "From that time Jesus began to preach and to say, 'Repent, for the kingdom of heaven is at hand'" (Matt. 4:17 NKJV).

William Temple insisted that "repentance does not mean merely giving up a bad habit." It means getting "a new mind":

> We have lowered the term "repentance" into meaning something not very different from remorse, though, of course, we all are aware that it is not true repentance unless the wrongdoing is abandoned. . . . Repentance does not mean merely giving up a bad habit. What it is concerned with is the mind; get a new mind. What mind? The mind of Christ—our standard of reference; learn to look at the world in His way.*

Seventeenth-century philosopher Blaise Pascal said, "We can only know God well when we know our own sin. And those who have known God without knowing their wretchedness have not glorified Him, but have glorified themselves."†

---

* Sulon G. Ferree, arr. and ed., *Selections from the Writings of William Temple* (Nashville, TN: The Upper Room, 1968), 12–13.
† Sherwood E. Wirt, ed., *Spiritual Disciplines: Devotional Writings from the Great Christian Leaders of the Seventeenth Century*, Christian Heritage Classics (Wheaton, IL: Crossway Books, 1983), 19.

It's very important—knowing our sin. It's in knowing our sin that a healthy guilt and a healthy shame will lead us to constructive change. The psalmist prayed: "Examine me, O Lord, and try me; test my mind and my heart" (Ps. 26:2 NASB1995). If we do not allow the Lord to examine us in this way, we become prisoners of our sin; we also set ourselves up for a pervasive guilt and shame that will continually mar our lives.

To know our sin doesn't mean that we have to wallow in it. We must trust the Lord; we must accept for ourselves the gift of salvation. In the very depth of our being we must claim the promise of Scripture: "If we confess our sins, he [Jesus] is faithful and just to forgive our sins and to cleanse us from all unrighteousness" (1 John 1:9 ESV). That's the beginning point of overcoming guilt and shame—knowing our sin, but not wallowing in it.

Temple speaks a challenging and encouraging word as he considers the condition of "being sorry for" as a dimension of repentance: "In itself, far from being sorrowful, [repentance] is the most joyful thing in the world, because when you have done it you have adopted the viewpoint of truth itself, and you are in fellowship with God."*

---

* Ferree, *Writings of William Temple*, 13.

REFLECTIVE MOMENT: Ponder Pascal's word: "We can only know God well when we know our own sin. And those who have known God without knowing their wretchedness have not glorified Him, but have glorified themselves."[*]

PRAYER: "Examine me, O LORD, and try me; test my mind and my heart."[†] Amen.

---

* Wirt, ed., *Spiritual Disciplines*, 19.
† Psalm 26:2 NASB1995.

DAY 33
William Temple

~~~

The Primacy of Love

If I speak in the tongues of men or of angels, but do not have love, I am only a resounding gong or a clanging cymbal. If I have the gift of prophecy and can fathom all mysteries and all knowledge, and if I have a faith that can move mountains, but do not have love, I am nothing. If I give all I possess to the poor and give over my body to hardship that I may boast, but do not have love, I gain nothing. (1 Cor. 13:1–3)

Many a poet, prose writer, essayist, scholar, preacher, and singer, reading Paul's magnificent hymn of love, has felt even if they haven't verbalized it: "I wish I had said that."

And all of us, reading it, want to exclaim, "Aha! That's it!"

Chapter 13 of Paul's First Letter to the Corinthians is his exposition of love, expressed poetically, but leaving nothing out. Our souls resonate with it because it is truth we have experienced, or need desperately to experience. With extraordinary understanding and clarity, with unmuddied sensitivity and spiritual depth, Paul has mined the very essence of the Christian gospel. Wherever Christians gather to worship and proclaim the gospel, 1 Corinthians 13 is known and loved.

This hymn is Paul's exposition of the meaning of *agape*, the New Testament word for Christian love. I would not pretend to clarify one of the most transparent expressions of truth in the Bible. All the saints with whom I "kept company" have spoken of love in one way or another.*

William Temple talks about love from two different perspectives. The first of those is *the victory of love*. He begins by asking: What is the driving power of progress? He responds:

> The natural man thinks it can be accomplished by force. But force alone achieves nothing positive, *because it does not convert the heart and will*. . . . There are in the world two kinds of Victory. One is the Victory of Pride or Self-assertion, which consists in imposing on the conquered the will of the conqueror. In such victory there is no peace; there is the bitterness of defeat, the hope of revenge, the renewal of the conflict when resources permit. And there is the Victory of Love—the only kind of victory with which God is content. Here there is no defeated party, for the victory consists in

---

* Maxie Dunnam, *The Workbook on Keeping Company with the Saints* (Nashville, TN: Upper Room, 2001).

the conversion of enemies into friends. The means to this victory is not force, but sacrifice. . . .

For the community which are freely to serve is, the last resort, the human race itself. . . . It is thus . . . that we can bring eternity into history, and work, as we pray, for the coming of God's perfect sovereignty.[*]

Though what he is saying this does apply to, and has political implications, Temple is quick to say that in the transformation of life in response to love, the chief requirement is not legislation by the state but a true conversion of individuals.

The second perspective from which Temple talks about the primacy of love is his conviction that *eternal life is the life of love.*

For the self-centered spirit there can be no eternal life. Even if it should exist for ever, its existence could only be an ever deepening chill of death. Because it seeks its satisfaction in itself, where none is to be found, it must suffer an always intenser pang of spiritual hunger, which cannot be allayed until that spirit turns to another source of satisfaction.[†]

I sat with a young woman not long ago to whom life had dealt a tragic blow. An uncaring husband had walked all over her— trampled her feelings, her very heart, in the mud. She had given

---

[*] Sulon G. Ferree, arr. and ed., *Selections from the Writings of William Temple* (Nashville, TN: The Upper Room, 1968), 20–21, italics added.
[†] Ferree, *Writings of William Temple*, 22.

herself to him, and he had used her. It was a despicable kind of harshness on his part.

It would have been a normal thing for her to be bitter, angry, calloused, and hard. The pain was there, and she wept a lot—but there was a tenderness about her, a kind of transparent perception of reality that defied reason, and she put it in a few words: "This is not the end for me—though I'm beaten down and crushed. This is not the end for me, because I know I am loved by God."

We need to get ahold of that truth for ourselves. Love is the heartbeat of God, and eternal life is the life of love.

REFLECTIVE MOMENT: How are you expressing love to those closest around you?

PRAYER: Give me strength, Lord, to overcome my self-centered spirit, and allow love to pervade my relationships with others. Amen.

DAY 34
Martin Luther

⟳

A Gracious God

"Now I commit you to God and to the word of his grace, which can build you up and give you an inheritance among all those who are sanctified." (Acts 20:32)

As I have indicated in many ways and in many places, for some time one of my spiritual disciplines has been keeping company with the saints. I have shared the rich treasure and learning from that in two workbooks: *Keeping Company with the Saints* and *Lessons from the Saints*. In *Lessons*, I shared and reflected on the ten characteristics I discovered common with the saints with whom I had kept company.

The first two characteristics that caught my attention were: *they passionately sought the Lord* and *they discovered a gracious God.* Martin Luther witnessed explicitly to this. In his soul learning, he vividly expressed these two lessons:

I am seeking, searching, thirsting for nothing else than a gracious God. Yet God continuously and earnestly offers himself as a God of grace, and urges even those who spurn him and are his enemies, to accept him as such.[*]

All the saints with whom I have kept company passionately sought God. This passion led them to work constantly at knowing God better and deeper.

Martin Luther is a household name in Protestant Christianity. Most books of Christian history include the story of his Ninety-Five Theses tacked to the door of the All Saints' Church. There is a sense he was the father of the Protestant Reformation.

When we think about him, the doctrine of *justification by faith* immediately comes to mind.

The Reformation, in which Martin Luther played so famous a part, was more than a revolt against the Roman Catholic ecclesiastical organization. It was a spiritual movement, quickening piety and calling to life many of the latent dispositions of the soul. . . .

[He] was not only able to think great thoughts; he had the happy facility of making plain what he thought to the understanding of others.[†]

---

[*] James Atkinson, ed., *Daily Readings with Martin Luther* (Springfield, IL: Templegate Publishers, 1987), 48.

[†] William R. Cannon, arr. and ed., *Table-Talk by Martin Luther* (Nashville, TN: The Upper Room, 1950), 3.

He put at the center of his classic *justification by grace through faith* the fact of a gracious God who gives himself to us:

> All the many countless blessings which God gives us here on earth are merely those gifts which last for a time. But his grace and loving regard are the inheritance which endures throughout eternity. . . . In giving us such gifts here on earth he is giving us only those things which are his own, but *in his grace and love toward us he gives his very self.* In receiving his gifts we touch but his hand; in his gracious regard we receive his heart, his spirit, his mind, his will.
>
> Man receives grace immediately and fully. In this way he is saved. Good works are not necessary to assist him in this: they follow. It is as if God were to produce a fresh, green tree out of a dry log, which tree would then bear its natural fruit.*

The gracious God and the Cross are intimately connected . . . the Cross, God's gift of his Son for our salvation. Likewise, the Cross is intimately connected with being Christian. Jesus' death on the cross and his call to deny ourselves, take up his cross daily and follow him are the heart of the Christian faith, spirituality, and discipleship. Luther could not have expressed it more solidly: "He who is not *crucianus,* if I may coin a word, is not

---

* Cannon, *Table-Talk with Martin Luther,* 49, italics mine.

Christianus: in other words, he who does not bear his cross is no Christian, for he is not like his Master, Jesus Christ."[*]

REFLECTIVE MOMENT: How does your understanding and experience of God harmonize with the experience of *a gracious God*?

PRAYER: Our Father in heaven, shape my mind and heart more and more to experience You as my *gracious Father*. Amen.

---

[*] Robert Llewelyn, ed., *The Joy of the Saints: Spiritual Readings throughout the Year* (Springfield, IL: Templegate Publishers, 1988), 258.

DAY 35
Martin Luther

∽

Conformed to the Likeness of Christ

Then they asked him, "What must we do to do the works God requires?"

Jesus answered, "The work of God is this: to believe in the one he has sent."

So they asked him, "What sign then will you give that we may see it and believe you? What will you do? Our ancestors ate the manna in the wilderness; as it is written: 'He gave them bread from heaven to eat.'"

Jesus said to them, "Very truly I tell you, it is not Moses who has given you the bread from heaven, but it is my Father who gives you the true bread from heaven. For the bread of God is the bread that comes down from heaven and gives life to the world."

"Sir," they said, "always give us this bread."

Then Jesus declared, "I am the bread of life. Whoever comes to me will never go hungry, and whoever believes in me will never be thirsty." (John 6:28–35)

Yesterday we shared Luther's claim that "he who does not bear his cross is no Christian, for he is not like his Master, Jesus Christ."* Jesus's death on the cross and His call to deny ourselves and take up His cross daily and follow Him are the heart of the Christian faith, spirituality, and discipleship. Luther talked about this idea in terms of being conformed to the likeness of Christ.

The cross teaches us to believe in hope even when there is no hope. The wisdom of the cross is deeply hidden in a profound mystery. In fact, Luther insisted:

> [T]here is no other way to heaven than taking up the cross of Christ. On account of this we must beware that the active life with its good works, and the contemplative life with its speculations, do not lead us astray. Both are attractive and yield peace of mind, but for that reason they hide real dangers, unless they are tempered by the cross and disturbed by adversaries. The cross is the surest path of all. Blessed is the man who understands this truth.†

I remember the chorus to a gospel hymn we sang in my early years as a Christian:

> Are you living in the shadow of the cross
> Where the Savior took your place?

---

* Robert Llewelyn, ed., *The Joy of the Saints: Spiritual Readings throughout the Year* (Springfield, IL: Templegate Publishers, 1988), 258.
† Llewelyn, ed., *The Joy of the Saints*, 258.

By the cross He'll lead us to that home above,

Where we'll see Him face to face.*

The liturgical season of Lent is the occasion when we Christians rehearse the passion, suffering, and death of our Lord Jesus. We who follow Jesus ought always to live *in the shadow of the cross.*

A Christian should not go to Jerusalem without deliberately walking the Via Dolorosa—the way that Jesus walked from the place of trial and sentencing to Golgotha, where He died that we might live. The stations of the cross are designated along the Via Dolorosa, marking the happenings on that long trek up Golgotha's hill. As I walked that way on my last visit, the most meaningful station for me was the one that marks the place where Jesus stumbled and fell. Roman soldiers looked out on the crowd of pilgrims packed into that narrow street, saw a big strong black man, Simon of Cyrene, and "pressed [him] into service"—that of bearing the cross of Jesus on to the place of crucifixion (Mark 15:21 NASB1995).

Think about it. No other person ever helped carry the actual cross upon which Jesus was crucified. What a notation for Simon's biographical sketch! But think more deeply as you think and respond to Jesus. Christians are to live as though on the Via Dolorosa because the call of Christ is a constant call to deny ourselves, take up His cross daily, and follow Him.

---

* "In the Shadow of the Cross," lyrics by Bernice M. Brostrom, music by Wesley H. Daniel, © 1938, renewed 1966 by Stamps-Baxter Music Company.

REFLECTIVE MOMENT: In what way are you being conformed to the likeness of Christ? Are you living in the shadow of the cross?

PRAYER: Lord Jesus, give me a stronger will to live in the shadow of the cross, that I might be a servant in Your style. Amen.

Martin Luther

 ⸺ ⟿ ⸺

God's Breathed Word

All Scripture is God-breathed and is useful for teaching, rebuking, correcting and training in righteousness, so that the servant of God may be thoroughly equipped for every good work. (2 Tim. 3:16–17)

George Gallup died in 1984 at age eighty-two. For more than fifty-five years he had studied American opinions and attitudes. One of his interests was exploring the inner life of people. He cited six basic spiritual needs of Americans. Number five in that list was *the need to know that one is growing in his or her faith.*

This is in harmony with the lessons I have learned from the saints: they practiced discipline, they believed obedience was essential, and they thirsted for holiness. These characteristics grew out of their immersion in Scripture.

John Wesley described himself as a "man of one book," and prayed, "Oh, give me that book." Luther declared:

> The Holy Scripture is the highest and best of books, abounding in comfort under all afflictions and trials. It teaches us to see, to feel, to grasp, and to comprehend faith, hope and charity, far otherwise than mere human reason can; and when evil oppresses us, it teaches us how these virtues throw light on the darkness, and how, after this poor miserable existence of ours on earth, there is another and an eternal life.[*]

The saints were aware of the need to know that one is growing in his or her faith. They responded to Paul's admonition: "As therefore you received Christ Jesus the Lord, so live in him, rooted and built up in him and established in the faith" (Col. 2:6–7a RSV).

The point is clear: after we have accepted Jesus Christ as Savior, we spend the rest of our lives bringing every aspect of our lives under the lordship of Jesus Christ. That means we choose to grow, to become stronger in our faith.

Luther admonished us about how we should see and respond to Scripture as a guide to and source of growth: "We ought not to

---

[*] James Atkinson, ed., *Daily Readings with Martin Luther* (Springfield, IL: Templegate Publishers, 1987), 5.

criticize, explain, or judge the Scriptures by our mere reason, but diligently, with prayer, meditate thereon, and seek their meaning."*

Then he added what, for me, is a surprising word:

> The devil and temptation afford us occasion to learn and understand the Scriptures, by experience and practice. Without these we should never understand them, however diligently we read and listen to them. The Holy Ghost must here be our only master and tutor.†

Scripture puts it this way: "Thy word is a lamp unto my feet, and a light unto my path" (Ps. 119:105 KJV). So register this fact clearly: when our minds are open to understand Scripture, our hearts are open to receive God's grace. The Bible is the primary channel through which God's grace comes.

Then there is this second truth: when our hearts are open to receive God's grace, our wills are softened to do God's bidding. Get the movement now. When our minds are open to understand the Scripture, our hearts are open to receive God's grace. And when our hearts are open to receive God's grace, our wills are softened to do God's bidding.

Now I know it's easier to use Bible language than to obey Bible commands. It has to do with whether our obedience is still

---

* Atkinson, *Daily Readings with Martin Luther,* 5.
† Atkinson, *Daily Readings with Martin Luther,* 5.

law-centered or grace-centered. The growth that comes from studying God's Word, from immersing ourselves in Scripture, moves us more and more to graceful living out of grateful response.

REFLECTIVE MOMENT: In what ways are you growing in your faith?

PRAYER: Holy Spirit, reveal to me the areas of my life that I need most to grow. Amen.

John Wesley

༼ ༽

Degrees in Faith

Instead, speaking the truth in love, we will grow to become in every respect the mature body of him who is the head, that is, Christ. From him the whole body, joined and held together by every supporting ligament, grows and builds itself up in love, as each part does its work. (Eph. 4:15–16)

John Wesley was a "son of the Church," born in the Church of England rectory at Epworth, England, on June 17, 1703. His life and ministry almost spanned the century; he died on March 2, 1791.

Most people in the Methodist/Wesleyan tradition of the Christian faith know at least the broad outline of Wesley's life. In 1725, having been nurtured by his mother, Susanna, and his father, Samuel, a priest in the Church of England, John, while a student at Oxford University, had a conversion to the ideal of holy living. There are few examples in history of a more disciplined religious person: he rose at 4:00 a.m., read the New Testament in Greek for an hour,

and then prayed for an hour with his brother Charles and others who
had joined him in what was derisively called the Holy Club. He spent
time visiting prisons and gave to the poor all of his money except
that which was absolutely necessary for his own living. He was a
person desperately seeking salvation and assurance of his salvation.

We have wonderful records of his ministry in the sermons he
preached, and in his journals and letters. He was a disciplined journal
writer and an avid correspondent; eight volumes of his journaling
and at least 2,600 of his letters have been preserved. These journals
and letters are the sources used for two of the booklets in the Great
Devotional Classics series. Rightly, Wesley joins the line of persons
who continue to inspire, challenge, and shape our Christian walk.

Wesley was a champion of plain religion: "Let *my* religion be
plain, artless, simple! Meekness, temperance, patience, faith, and
love, be these *my* highest gifts; and let the highest words wherein I
teach them be those I learn from the book of God!"*

Throughout his ministry he was concerned about what he labeled
"Almost Christian." On May 16, 1753, he wrote to Ebenezer Blackwell:

> I have often observed with a sensible pleasure your strong
> desires to be not almost only but altogether a Christian. And
> what should hinder it? What is it that prevents those good

---

* Paul Lambourne Higgins, arr. and ed., *Selections from the Journal
of John Wesley* (Nashville, TN: The Upper Room, 1967), 14, italics in
original.

desires from being brought to good effect? Is it carrying a right principle too far? I mean, a desire to please all men for their good? Or is it a kind of shame? the being ashamed not of sin but of holiness, or of what conduces thereto? . . . I have often been afraid that you do not gain ground in this respect; nay, that you rather go backward by yielding to this than forward by conquering it. I have feared that you are not so bold for God now as you were four or five years ago. If so, you are certainly in great danger.*

Wesley referred to himself as a "man of one book." Throughout his life he took Paul's word to the Ephesian church to heart, that "we will grow to become in every respect the mature body of him who is the head, that is, Christ" (Eph. 4:15). He wrote of this in his journal:

There are degrees in faith, and [I believe] that a man may have some degree of it before all things in him are become new—before he has the same assurance of faith, the abiding witness of the Spirit, or the clear perception that Christ dwelleth in him.

Accordingly, I believe there is a degree of justifying faith (and consequently a state of justification) short of, and commonly antecedent to this.

* J. Manning Potts, arr. and ed., *Selections from the Letters of John Wesley* (Nashville, TN: The Upper Room, 1952), 25.

I believe the way to attain it is to wait for Christ and be still in using all the means of grace.*

Worship, fasting, prayer, the Lord's Supper, baptism, and Scripture were the means of grace Wesley mentioned most often.

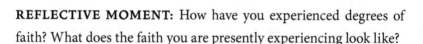

REFLECTIVE MOMENT: How have you experienced degrees of faith? What does the faith you are presently experiencing look like?

PRAYER: Lord, when I begin to fret too much about my faith and become anxious, strengthen my will to practice Your will today and rely on Your grace. Amen.

---

* Higgins, *Journal of John Wesley*, 14.

John Wesley

ༀ

Going on to Salvation

This righteousness is given through faith in Jesus Christ to all who believe. There is no difference between Jew and Gentile, for all have sinned and fall short of the glory of God, and all are justified freely by his grace through the redemption that came by Christ Jesus. (Rom. 3:22–24)

The prevailing emphasis of Scripture was, likewise, Wesley's prevailing emphasis. However, he did not put the emphasis solely on our coming into the Christian life in confessing, repenting, and trusting Christ as Savior and receiving forgiveness.

Wesley's understanding was broader. He used the term *salvation* to refer to the entire saving activity of God in human lives. Thus, in the Methodist/Wesleyan tradition, we talk about "going on to salvation."

In a letter to his brother Samuel on October 30, 1738, he wrote:

Dear Brother,—With regard to my own character, and my doctrine likewise, I shall answer you plainly. By a Christian I mean one who so believes in Christ as that sin hath no more dominion over him; and in this obvious sense of the word I was not a Christian till May the 24th last past. For till then sin had the dominion over me, although I fought with it continually; but surely then, from that time to this it hath not—such is the free grace of God in Christ.*

Saints alive! In Wesley's mind and experience, there was *full salvation*.

The two pivotal dynamics of full salvation are justification and sanctification. Both are works of grace. In justification, we are pardoned and reconciled to God; the restoration of the image of God in us is begun, which is the beginning of sanctification.

Justification may be the miracle of a moment, but sanctification is the process of a lifetime.

The dynamic process of sanctification is to work out in fact what is already true in principle. In *position*, in our relationship to God in Jesus Christ, we are new persons; that is justification and new birth. Now our *condition*, the actual

---

* J. Manning Potts, arr. and ed., *Selections from the Letters of John Wesley* (Nashville, TN: The Upper Room, 1952), 7.

life we live, must be brought into harmony with our new
position. That is the process of sanctification.*

Justification, the new birth, is the starting point of sanctification.

I believe [the new birth] to be an inward thing; a change from
inward wickedness to inward goodness; an entire change of
our inmost nature from the image of the devil (wherein we
are born) to the image of God; a change from the love of the
creature to the love of the Creator; from earthly and sensual
to heavenly and holy affections,—in a word, a change from
the tempers of the spirit of darkness to those of the angels of
God in heaven.†

Over and over, in his journal, he confirmed personal testimony
of salvation working in the lives of believers.

The barber who shaved me said, "Sir, I praise God on your
behalf. When you was at Bolton last, I was one of the most
eminent drunkards in all the town; but I came to listen at the
window, and God struck me to the heart. I then earnestly
prayed for the power against drinking; and God gave me

* Maxie Dunnam, *Going on to Salvation: A Study in the Wesleyan
Tradition* (Nashville, TN: Discipleship Resources, 1996), 42.
† Paul Lambourne Higgins, arr. and ed., *Selections from the Journal of
John Wesley* (Nashville, TN: The Upper Room, 1967), 9.

more than I asked: He took away the very desire of it. Yet I felt myself worse and worse, till, on the 5th of April last, I could hold out no longer. I knew I must drop into hell that moment unless God appeared to save me. And He did appear. I knew He loved me, and felt sweet peace. Yet I did not dare to say I had faith, till yesterday was twelve-month, God gave me faith; and His love has ever since filled my heart."[*]

Whereas in his early struggles to be Christian, Wesley practiced discipline in order to become a Christian, going on to salvation he experienced joy in being Christian by practicing disciplines that once had been a drudgery. In the societies that were established and became a part of this emerging Methodist movement, social service, especially with the poor, became standard.

I reminded the United Society that many of our brethren and sisters had not needful food; many were destitute of convenient clothing; many were out of business, and that without their own fault; and many sick and ready to perish; that I had done what in me lay to feed the hungry, to clothe the naked, to employ the poor, and to visit the sick; but was not, alone, sufficient for these things, and therefore desired all whose hearts were as my heart:

1. To bring what clothes each could spare, to be distributed among those that wanted most.

---

[*] Higgins, *Journal of John Wesley*, 10.

2. To give weekly a penny, or what they could afford, for the relief of the poor and sick.

My design, I told them, is to employ, for the present, all the women who are out of business, and desire it, in knitting.

To these we will first give the common price for what work they do; and then add, according to their need.*

⌒

REFLECTIVE MOMENT: Considering Wesley's understanding, what aspects of full salvation are missing in your life? Are you going on to salvation?

PRAYER: Eternal God, open our minds and hearts to the glorious awareness of Your presence. By Your Holy Spirit, guide our going on to salvation. Amen.

---

* Higgins, *Journal of John Wesley*, 20–21.

DAY 39
John Wesley

— ᗢ —

Assurance and Perfection

The Spirit himself testifies with our spirit that we are God's children. Now if we are children, then we are heirs—heirs of God and co-heirs with Christ, if indeed we share in his sufferings in order that we may also share in his glory. (Rom. 8:16–17)

"Be perfect, therefore, as your heavenly Father is perfect." (Matt. 5:48)

Assurance and perfection are cardinal dimensions of Wesley's teaching. We can have the assurance of our salvation and our ultimate calling: perfection, or holiness.

The most classic witness of Wesley was his testimony to assurance:

In the evening I went very unwillingly to a society in Aldersgate Street, where one was reading Luther's preface to the *Epistle to the Romans*. About a quarter before nine, while he was describing the change which God works in the heart through faith in Christ, I felt my heart strangely warmed. I felt I did trust in Christ, Christ alone for salvation; and an assurance was given me that He had taken away *my* sins, even *mine*, and saved *me* from the law of sin and death.

I began to pray with all my might for those who had in a more especial manner despitefully used me and persecuted me. I then testified openly to all there what I now first felt in my heart. But it was not long before the enemy suggested, "This cannot be faith; for where is thy joy?" Then was I taught that peace and victory over sin are essential to faith in the Captain of our salvation; but that, as to the transports of joy that usually attend the beginning of it, especially in those who have mourned deeply, God sometimes giveth, sometimes withholdeth them, according to the counsels of His own will.

After my return home, I was much buffeted with temptations; but I cried out, and they fled away. They returned again and again. I as often lifted up my eyes, and He "sent me help from His holy place." And herein I found the difference between this and my former state chiefly consisted. I was striving, yea, fighting with all my might under the law, as well as under grace. But then I was sometimes, if not often, conquered; now, I was always conqueror.*

* Paul Lambourne Higgins, arr. and ed., *Selections from the Journal of John Wesley* (Nashville, TN: The Upper Room, 1967), 8–9, italics in original.

Wesley was a man desperately seeking salvation and assurance of his salvation. In a despondent mood because his struggles were providing no peace, he went to the prayer meeting and had the watershed experience that gave him the assurance of salvation. Naturally, this became a part of his teaching. Saints alive! Assurance is the privilege of every Christian; all persons can know they are saved, and they can be saved to the uttermost. For Wesley this meant "Christian perfection," another term for sanctification.

There must have been confusion among his followers about this issue, because he wrote his brother Charles a lengthy letter, seeking understanding and agreement.

Dear Brother,—Some thoughts occurred to my mind this morning which I believe may be useful to set down: the rather because it may be a means of our understanding each other clearly; that we may agree as far as ever we can and then let all the world know it.

I was thinking of Christian Perfection, with regard to the thing, the manner, and the time.

1. By perfection I mean the humble, gentle, patient love of God ruling all the tempers, words, and actions, the whole heart by the whole life. I do not include an impossibility of falling from it, either in part or in whole. . . . I do not contend for the term sinless, though I do not object to it. . . .

2. As to the manner, I believe this perfection is always wrought in the soul by faith, consequently in an instant. But

I believe in as gradual work both preceding and following that instant.*

For Wesley, the terms *Christian perfection, sanctification,* and *holiness* carried the same meaning. Saints alive! Holiness is not optional for Christians. Jesus was forthright: "You shall be perfect, just as your Father in heaven is perfect" (Matt. 5:48 NJKV). The Holy Spirit, through inspiration given to Peter, confirms the call: "As He who called you *is* holy, you also be holy in all *your* conduct" (1 Peter 1:15 NKJV).

For Wesley, the whole of salvation and the Christian life was all grace, and the power of the Holy Spirit, accessed through undoubting prayer and surrender.

The day after his Aldersgate experience, he wrote in his journal:

The moment I awaked, "Jesus, Master," was in my heart and in my mouth; and I found all my strength lay in keeping my eye fixed upon him, and my soul waiting on him continually. Being again at St. Paul's in the afternoon, I could taste the good word of God in the anthem which began, "My song shall be always of the loving kindness of the Lord: With my mouth will I ever be showing forth thy truth from one generation to another." Yet the enemy injected a fear, "If thou dost believe, why is there not a more sensible change?"

---

* J. Manning Potts, arr. and ed., *Selections from the Letters of John Wesley* (Nashville, TN: The Upper Room, 1952), 26–27.

I answered ... "That I know not. But this I know, I have now 'peace with God.'" And I sin not today, and Jesus my master has forbid me to take no thought of the morrow.*

～

REFLECTIVE MOMENT: Do you have assurance of your salvation? Has holiness been a part of the teaching of your church? What does sanctification mean to you?

PRAYER: Loving Father, thank You for this opportunity to consider the great devotional classics. Let me not forget that great resources are available for my devotional life and development. Lead me to those who will lead me in my ongoing relationship with You. I desire a closer walk. Amen.

---

* *The Works of John Wesley*, vol. 1 (Grand Rapids, MI: Zondervan, 1872), 104.

DAY 40
John Calvin

⸏

Prayer at the Heart of Our Discipline

I appeal to you therefore, brothers and sisters, by the mercies
of God, to present your bodies as a living sacrifice, holy and
acceptable to God, which is your spiritual worship. Do not be
conformed to this world, but be transformed by the renewing of
your minds, so that you may discern what is the will of God—
what is good and acceptable and perfect. (Rom. 12:1–2 NRSVCE)

As mentioned on day 34, the first of the ten characteristics
of the saints are: *they passionately sought the Lord* and *they
discovered a gracious God.* The second characteristic is *they practice
discipline, with prayer at its heart.* Saints alive! What an appropriate
way to close our forty-day pilgrimage—with attention to prayer at
the heart of our discipline as a means of grace.

At our best, in the Methodist/Wesleyan tradition, we have an
equal and zealous emphasis on personal and social holiness. Our

founder, John Wesley, said, "As tenacious of inward holiness as a mystic, of outward holiness as a Pharisee."*

That is a picture we can live with and build upon. It's a picture to hold in our minds, as we think about the place of discipline in the Christian life. For more than forty years, in my teaching and preaching, I have defined spiritual formation as the dynamic process of receiving through faith and appropriating through commitment, discipline, and action the living Christ into our own life to the end that our life will conform to and manifest the reality of Christ's presence in the world.

Mother Teresa painted the picture clearly in her confession: "Pray for me that I not loosen my grip on the hands of Jesus even under the guise of ministering to the poor."† Paul's word to the Romans in our scripture today makes it clear.

The saints with whom I have kept company practiced discipline with prayer at the heart of it. John Calvin states:

> We clearly see how completely destitute man is of all good, how devoid of every means of procuring his own salvation. Hence, if he would obtain succor in his necessity, he must go beyond himself, and procure it in some other quarter. It has been farther shown, that the Lord kindly and spontaneously

---

* John Wesley, "On God's Vineyard," *Works*, vol. 7, 205.
† Richard J. Foster, "The Celebration of Meditative Prayer," *Christianity Today*, October 7, 1983, https://www.christianitytoday.com/ct/1983/october-7/celebration-of-meditative-prayer.html.

manifests Himself in Christ, in whom He offers all happiness for our misery, all abundance for our want, opening up the treasure of heaven to us, so that we may turn with full faith to His beloved Son, depend upon Him with full expectation, rest in Him and cleave to Him with full hope.*

Calvin sounded some rules of Christian prayer:

First, "to have our heart and mind framed as becomes those who are entering into converse with God."

Two, "in asking we must always truly feel our wants, and seriously considering that we need all the things which we ask, accompany the prayer with a sincere, nay ardent, desire of obtaining them."

Three, "divest himself of all vain-glorious thoughts, lay aside all idea of worth . . . humbly giving God the whole glory, lest by arrogating anything, however little, to himself, vain pride cause Him to turn away His face."

Four, "abased and truly humble, we should be animated to pray with the sure hope of succeeding."†

Saints alive! What a word with which to close our pilgrimage with the saints.

Since no man is worthy to come forward in his own name, and appear in the presence of the heavenly Father, to relieve

---

* Norman Victor Hope, arr. and ed., *Selections from the Writings of John Calvin* (Nashville, TN: The Upper Room, 1958), 13.
† Hope, *Writings of John Calvin*, 16–18.

us at once from fear and shame, with which we must all feel oppressed, has given us His Son, Jesus Christ our Lord, to be our Advocate and Mediator, that under His guidance we may approach securely, confident that with Him for our Intercessor nothing which we ask in His name will be denied to us, as there is nothing which the Father can deny to Him.[*]

—————————————— ∽ ——————————————

REFLECTIVE MOMENT: What plans do you have for moving forward on your Christian walk?

PRAYER: Oh Master, give me the will and the willingness to walk with You, wherever You lead. Amen.

—————————

[*] Hope, *Writings of John Calvin*, 18.